Whackademia

Richard Hil is an academic and writer who has worked at several universities in Australia and the UK and is currently honorary associate at the Centre for Peace and Conflict Studies, University of Sydney. His latest books include *Erasing Iraq: The Human Costs of Carnage* (with Mike Otterman and Paul Wilson, 2010) and the edited collection *Surviving Care: Achieving Justice and Healing for the Forgotten Australians* (with Liz Branigan, 2010), and he has published articles about issues in higher education for *The Australian*, *Campus Review* and *Australian Universities Review*.

Whackademia

An insider's account of the troubled university

RICHARD HIL

NEWSOUTH

A NewSouth book

NewSouth Publishing
University of New South Wales Press Ltd
University of New South Wales
Sydney NSW 2052
AUSTRALIA
newsouthpublishing.com

First published 2012
10 9 8 7 6 5 4 3 2 1

National Library of Australia
Cataloguing-in-Publication entry
Author: Hil Richard, 1953–
Title: Whackademia: An insider's account of the troubled university/Richard Hil.
ISBN: 978 1 74223 291 1 (pbk.)
ISBN: 978 1 74224 136 4 (ePub)
ISBN: 978 1 74224 347 4 (Kindle)
ISBN: 978 1 74224 586 7 (ePDF)
Subjects: Universities and colleges – Social aspects – Australia.
College environment – Australia.
Dewey Number: 378.00994

Design Di Quick
Cover design Xou Creative
Printer Griffin Press

This book is printed on paper using fibre supplied from plantation or sustainably managed forests.

Contents

Acknowledgments

My thanks go to all those academics who took time out to talk to me about their university experiences. I have done my best to conceal your identities but there's really no need to worry: a lot of other academics are saying exactly the same sorts of things! I would also like to thank Phillipa McGuinness, Executive Publisher at UNSW Press, for her patience and support throughout this project, and James Drown for his amazing editing skills. My gratitude also goes to the anonymous reviewer for his or her comments – they certainly helped, and I hope you like the book a little better now! Last but not least, my heartfelt thanks and appreciation go to Jennifer Grainger for her 'belt and braces' support in reading through the manuscript and picking up my usual foibles.

Introduction: Grounds for complaint

Working in a university is like being in a really bad British farce: lots of racing around with no clear direction.

SENIOR LECTURER IN EDUCATION, MELBOURNE

Academics have been reduced to administrators and facilitators of formulaic, googlised, dumbed-down education.

PROFESSOR OF POLITICAL SCIENCE, CANBERRA

Universities are knowledge department stores.

LINDSAY TANNER, FORMER FINANCE MINISTER AND NOW VICE CHANCELLOR'S FELLOW AT VICTORIA UNIVERSITY

Like most organisations in other industrial and commercial sectors – schools, hospitals, biscuit factories, banks and breweries – universities have over recent years experienced major changes to their workplace cultures. Australian academics are now subject to work regimes that few of their predecessors would have recognised barely thirty years ago. Economic rationalism, commercialisation, managerialism, corporate governance and other outgrowths of neo-liberal ideology have ushered in an entirely new way of thinking about what constitutes academic life, what universities are for, and what values these institutions represent.

The notion of universities as institutions for the collective good has been largely usurped by the need to survive in an increasingly cut-throat marketplace. The once stereotypical image of an academic – a middle-class, pipe-smoking patriarch with all the time in the world to contemplate lofty ideas – has been replaced by the current reality of workers immersed in the rush of corporate activity, mostly aimed at peddling their institutions' educational wares and maintaining market share. This change has been accompanied by bureaucratic practices and corporate jargon common to other sectors – inputs, outputs, targets, key performance indicators, performance management, unit costs, cost effectiveness, benchmarking, quality assurance and so on – that together form a system dedicated to maintaining corporate discipline, brand distinctiveness and market share.

And if educational 'products' like degrees, diplomas and PhDs are to be sold on the open market, then it is necessary to ensure an acquiescent and disciplined academic workforce, one that publicly supports the corporate line, protects the brand and fulfils the onerous duties required of it. Constant monitoring and surveillance – through regulatory mechanisms of review, assessment and evaluation – ensure that compliance is achieved under the guise of transparency, accountability and quality assurance. As academics have themselves reported in numerous newspaper articles and research studies, the net effects of this formidable regulatory order have been a perceived lowering of professional status, a sense of being constantly surveyed and swamped by red tape, and the loss of creative license, intellectual freedom and something called 'job satisfaction'. Needless to say, many academics also now report high levels of stress, depression and related anxiety disorders, as well as a desperate desire to flee the profession – a feeling most prevalent in Australia among the estimated reserve army of 67 000 casual employees who now represent about 60 per cent of the academic workforce.

Many academics also report that they cannot devote as much quality time as they would like to what they consider to be their most important activities – teaching and research – and that they waste considerable energy simply monitoring and reporting what they are doing, or grappling with the onerous demands of large numbers of needy students. Not surprisingly, this situation has led to a generalised state of existential malaise in which many disgruntled and disillusioned academics ponder what it means to be an academic in today's university system.

The story of my own twenty-five years of academic work in both British and Australian universities (related in chapter 1) is, I suspect, a fairly typical account of personal disenchantment with a system that has gradually mutated into its present corporate form. The sense of excitement and ideological fervor which initially propelled me into an academic career has since been eroded by a stifling sense of obligation to the survival of the largely joyless institutions in which I worked. It wasn't so much the drudgery of the business model that irked me – I found its application to the universities bemusing, mainly because it was administered so amateurishly. More disenchanting was the fact that many of my colleagues seemed so eager, or so easily resigned, to embracing it. I was constantly struck by how fellow academics in the arts and social sciences could teach courses involving 'critical reflection', yet remain so reluctant to apply such intellectual processes when confronting the questionable rationalities of today's universities.

Instead, what I witnessed was a tendency among my colleagues to embody aspects of the new order even though, in private, many would berate the corporatisation of universities and promise to revolt or get out as soon as possible. Others clung desperately to the moral raft of pragmatism – 'I have a mortgage and kids to support'; 'I'll never get a promotion if I cause trouble' – or confined their critiques to journal articles, books and occasional newsletters. Yet others chose resistance through their trade unions and/or acts of industrial sabotage – faking workload calculations and avoiding performance reviews – or equally as effective, applying heavy doses of satire and ridicule, examples of which litter the pages of this book. But many also seemed to think that the system was just dandy, and the more commercialisation and quality control the better. After all, they argued, we are in the real world and there is no alternative.

Altered states

Despite these differing reactions there was one development on which everyone agreed: the nature of 'academic' work had altered significantly over the years, radically transforming the profession's everyday activities. For instance, as time wore on I noticed that discussions in staff and other meetings tended to focus increasingly on workload allocations, attrition rates, grant acquisition and student enrolments, rather than any meaningful consideration of what we as academics were doing and why we were doing it. These vexed questions rarely surfaced in the new reality, other than to confirm the sector's links to the wonders of the global market. To make matters worse, class sizes and administrative loads blew out and faculty administrators and school heads were handed extraordinary powers over academics. In the midst of all this, many academics had gradually morphed into docile subjects or, worse, remunerated zombies.

Academics now ply their trade in a system that encourages hyperactivity, obsessively measures and standardises everything, and is hell-bent on attracting and retaining students. So entrenched have these instrumental concerns become that in some universities an academic's penchant for reading scholarly works or sitting in quiet contemplation during office hours is seen as a monumental waste of time. In short, today's academics find themselves in a strange, perplexing world of conflicting realities in which public claims of excellence seem starkly at odds with what routinely goes on inside the modern university. This is a world in which vice chancellors, like many other corporate CEOs, draw hefty salary packages, totalling over a million dollars in some cases, while the majority of those who do the hard graft of teaching – casual employees – struggle along with risible job security, remuneration and hefty workloads in what comes close to a system of patronage. It's also a world in which globe-trotting vice chancellors, deputy vice chancellors and pro vice chancellors occupy plush offices, supported and even sustained by a bevy of personal assistants and administrators, while academics take on increasing amounts of on-line teaching and administration. Meanwhile, eager marketing and promotion personnel invent tacky brand adverts that are plastered everywhere from newspapers and cinemas to billboards and the sides of taxis and public buses.

Equally worrying for academics is the fact that universities, and academics in particular, remain firmly in the grip of negative public mythology. There remains a widespread belief that academics have it good when compared to workers elsewhere. In some cases this is probably true. As many university administrators are fond of pointing out (however erroneously), academics seem to be conspicuously absent from university campuses from about November to January. These same finger-pointers also allude to the relatively small number of formal teaching hours of most academics (especially when compared to school and TAFE teachers) and holidays masquerading as overseas conference attendance as damning evidence that they are pampered and spoiled employees. But these are merely the soft-targets of modern academic life. Copious evidence shows that Australian academics confront often insurmountable workloads across the calendar year, and that this seriously impacts on their health and well-being, and ability to perform core duties. Yet very little public recognition of this will come from government ministers or vice chancellors – although some of the latter, like Professor Paul Greenfield, the former vice chancellor of the University of Queensland, Professor Greg Craven of the Australian Catholic University, and Professor Steven Schwartz at Macquarie University have at least tried to highlight serious educational and other deficiencies in the system, as well as the failure to present a clear view of what higher education is for.

It is as if academics have been shackled by the myths of the past, unable to get it across to a largely disinterested audience that their work demands are injurious to health, happiness and good education. As such, academics have become, at least in policy discourse, shadow figures in the public eye. This is a situation made all the worse by higher education commentators – including senior academics and government ministers – who make little or no mention of academics or the challenges they face in the current system.

But it's not only the cultural and structural aspects of professional work that concern academics. They also point to the effects these are having on the nature and quality of so-called higher education. As I note in later chapters, the rigid and formulaic approach to university teaching, with its links to economic and vocational imperatives, and despite all the latest expert teaching theories and technological wizardry, is in many cases delivering a narrow and low-grade education for their students. Numerous employers, and even some vice chancellors, have begun to complain, and complain bitterly, about the one-dimensional nature of modern university graduates.

As this book indicates, what worries many academics is how growing commercialisation and the constriction of curriculum content to suit certain vocational, market-orientated ends has impacted on how and what students learn – and ultimately upon their capacity to become active citizens in a thriving, participatory democracy. Many academics argue that instead of simply encouraging graduates to pursue their personal ambitions of career, job readiness, professional status and high salaries in a competitive market culture, the role of universities should be to develop pedagogical practices that produce more 'rounded', more globally aware and 'citizen-minded' students who subscribe to an ethic of the common good.

Marketplace academics

Despite the fact that universities continue to graduate students across a range of disciplines who go on to make important contributions in various walks of life, altered funding arrangements in Britain (where arts, humanities, social sciences, law and business courses will no longer receive government subsidies), the questioning and disappearance of liberal arts courses in some Australian universities, and the funnelling of funds to applied science research, have all signalled a shift to more hard-nosed economic priorities. Add to this the proliferation of business schools (many with questionable reputations), the teaching of what critical theorist David Harvey derides as free-market, capitalist economics, and the fact that today's architects of de-regulated tertiary education invariably equate higher education with economic growth, and it is not too difficult to see why universities have embarked on their current trajectory. Whatever the claims of university mandarins, it is clear that these institutions have become a constituent element in the market-driven ambitions of the neo-liberal state.

It is worth pausing at this stage to consider briefly what is meant by an 'academic'. According to the Commonwealth Department of Education, Employment and Workplace Relations (DEEWR) in 2010 there were just under 50 000 full-time and fractional full-time academic staff in Australian universities working in regional and metropolitan campuses across a range of disciplines. Over 31 000 of these undertook both teaching and research, slightly under 16 000 specialised in research, and a small crop of 2000 or so concentrated exclusively on teaching. As to what exactly is meant by an 'academic', there is simply no agreed definition. I have long thought – naively I'll admit – that academics mostly undertake research and publish their findings in scholarly outlets and then apply their insights in teaching situations and occasionally speak out on matters of public concern. They might do a bit of administration and community and professional service, but their focus is research and teaching.

I have come to learn, however, that none of these assumptions hold true in the current tertiary system. For instance, if we take teaching and research as our yardstick, then many of those who work in Australian universities would – despite the categorisations of DEEWR – probably not qualify as academics because many of them do little or no research. In some quarters, however, there is a push for more 'teaching only' positions, with the insistence that these employees are still 'academics' simply by virtue of the fact that they work in universities. On the other hand, casual employees, the majority of whom (around 57 per cent) are women in their thirties, do a lot of teaching – in fact, that's all that most of them do! Half or more of the tertiary teaching load, and up to 80 per cent in some courses, is done by casual staff, albeit with few if any of the benefits afforded to full-time academic staff.

While some academics do more teaching or research than others, all face the daily grind of over-administration – a major source of complaint amongst the nation's scholars, mainly because it impedes their ability to concentrate on activities such as teaching and research. Administration has taken on a life of its own in today's universities and is central to the maintenance of a system devoted to the delivery of a branded product called 'higher education'. But not any sort of education. Australian university education is delivered through a quasi-market mixture of public and private funding that is tethered to particular instrumental goals like job readiness, professional careers and the promise of hefty incomes. As consumers, or my preferred term, 'shoppers', students have come to expect a product – a degree, diploma or doctorate – that will equip them to compete for jobs in the employment marketplace. As noted, this equation between higher education and job orientation has been constantly reinforced by policy-makers and senior university advocates who draw links between higher education and productivity, the economy, economic growth and GDP, as if these were the only measures of success. Contributing to the economy, of course, means engaging in that world on its terms, including a commercial ethos that requires (as we shall see in chapter 2) the full promotional powers of marketing and public relations personnel, of which there is now a veritable army in the tertiary sector.

One of the keys aims of this enterprise is to keep income-garnering student-shoppers rolling through the doors in what, after the removal of government caps in 2012, will be one of the most de-regulated systems of higher education in the world. But while student-shopper numbers have begun to mushroom, the same is unlikely to be the case among permanent academic staff. In fact, full-time academics are a diminishing breed, outnumbered by a growing band of casual staff, administrators, and middle and senior managers who have become bit-players in mini-empires that constantly seek to expand their activities domestically and overseas through new courses, on-line services and swanky (actual and virtual) designer campuses.

Academics – continuing and otherwise – have also had to confront the realities of what has been termed 'massification', whereby increasingly large droves of student-shoppers have been elevated to the status of royalty. The most revered of these regal shoppers are the full-fee-paying overseas students, who provide about 18 per cent of student income to universities and, according to Access Economics, contributed $9.6 billion to the Australian economy in 2009. Unfortunately, large numbers from this premium clientele have dropped away over the past couple of years, mainly because of 'reputational issues' (like the bashings of Indian students and perceptions of poor-quality education), the over-valued Aussie dollar, and better value-for-money in other countries.

To offset what is a significant loss of income – and any ensuing institutional panic – the federal government in 2011 loosened visa restrictions, allowing overseas students more generous entry requirements and the possibility of two years of employment following graduation. Additionally, many universities significantly eased their student entry requirements, while others have begun to draw more and more funds from charitable donations, bequests and endowments. Some universities even employ their own students in call centres to hunt down funds from alumni in order to bolster institutional coffers, or have attempted to poach students from other universities – despite this being in breach of their own university rules.

Other universities have flogged off the equivalent of the Crown Jewels – buildings and, in the case of the University of Sydney, a painting by Picasso – to fund various infrastructure developments. Sydney, Monash, Macquarie and the University of Central Queensland have all taken the option of shedding both administrative and academic staff. Faced with a $36 million debt caused by the downturn in overseas student numbers, La Trobe University in Melbourne has also considered lay-offs, as well as imposing levies on those faculties which fail to meet their enrolment targets – an interesting variation of rubbing salt into the wound.

Given such developments, it is hardly surprising that academics are nervous about job security, which for casual staff is just about non-existent anyway. For the more permanent employees, the notion of tenure – once a cherished feature of scholarly life – is largely a thing of the past. Academics, like employees in other sectors, now find themselves vulnerable to the vagaries of market forces. In effect, this has served to act as yet another regulatory mechanism, helping to ensure that all remains relatively quiet on the academic front. Not that academics have remained quiet for long. Struggles over enterprise bargaining agreements, staff-room disputes and a generalised culture of disaffection and complaint has taken hold.

Purposeful complaint

Although this book records a lot of complaints about the things that academics find disagreeable, odd, boorish, stifling, restrictive, irritating and downright toxic in today's university system, it has a higher purpose: namely, to highlight the parlous state of Australia's higher education sector and the urgent need to do something about this.

Most people complain some or all of the time about their pay and conditions – it's a simple fact of working life. Some readers may nonetheless find it irksome that seemingly well-paid employees appear to be droning on about how hard their professional lives have become. But as mentioned above (and as I demonstrate in greater detail in later chapters) most of the academics who undertake teaching are in fact lowly-paid casual staff who share little or none of the job security held by their colleagues on continuing contracts. Many casual academics consider that the full-timers have it good when compared to themselves, and there is some truth in this when it comes to pay and conditions. But none of this discounts the altered realities of the work culture of *all* university academics, nor the fact that significant numbers of them find the current regime oppressive, overwhelming, injurious to health, and antithetical to their ideas of a scholarly life.

It is of course possible to find cases of both open resistance and blissful acceptance, but these are few and far between. The fact is – as evidenced in numerous research reports – complaint is rife among academics, even among apologists of the current system. Sometimes academics will complain nervously about work conditions during staff meetings, or more publicly at seminars and conferences. Complaints also arise in more measured terms in academic journals and books, of which there are a growing number highlighting the oddities of the university system. Such critical assaults have been aired in the United States by commentators like Richard Arum and Josipa Roksa, Louis Menand, and Martha Nussbaum; in Australia by Simon Cooper, Simon Marginson and Robert Manne; and in Britain by Frank Furedi, AC Grayling and Terry Eagleton who, among many others, provide important insights into the troubled soul of today's higher education system.

Importantly, these complainants are not just venting their collective spleens: they have demonstrable grounds for serious concern about the state of universities and the need for cultural and organisational change. The importance of their observations cannot be over-stated. As Julian Baggini points out in *Complaint: From Minor Moans to Principled Protest*, 'Complaint ... has driven human society forward and led to the abolition of systemic injustice. That it is now associated with inconsequential moans and frivolous litigation is a travesty.' Baggini describes complaint as 'a directed expression of a refusal or inability to accept that things are not as they ought to be. It plays a major role in the quest for fairness, justice, or simply doing things differently.'

Such expression is evident among large sections of the academic workforce for whom everyday university life has become an unpleasant chore that has directly affected their ability to carry out core duties and to remain content and happy. In fact in recent surveys by the National Tertiary Education Union (NTEU) and the Centre for the Study of Higher Education at the University of Melbourne, the majority felt this way. Their complaints are an amalgam of the general, unspecified and specific. The unspecified stuff, often delivered through gritted teeth at staff meetings and occasional rants that simply exhaust the complainant, seem destined to go nowhere. Somewhere along the line, complaint – if it is to have any meaning and impact – has to involve a reframing of the current reality; a vision of what might be, rather than what is. It has to recognise that everything cannot be achieved, and that we need to be (in that awful managerial vernacular) 'strategic'. Baggini argues that 'right complaint' should contain two overriding principles if it is to be effective: specificity and proportionality. Being specific suggests a clear target or object of complaint rather than a scattergun approach. Proportionality, on the other hand, reminds us of the many other 'big picture' issues that are constantly out there: war, poverty, hunger, disease, climate change and the like.

While not as specific or proportionate as Baggini might wish, the major complaint of this book is that Whackademia – the repressive and constricting work culture currently operating in our universities – has turned these institutions into functional, rather soulless commercial enterprises rather than places of passion, spark, spontaneity and curiosity relevant to a vibrant and truly engaged democratic society. These attributes have been largely buried beneath a rhetorical pile of turgid rationalist pursuits that kow-tow to the capitalist market. Market demand dictates everything inside universities, including which programs survive and which go to the wall. Raimond Gaita has noted that this 'betrayal by utilitarianism' has resulted in less rather than more choice, and has changed the character of university education from civic relevance to instrumental economy.

Equally concerning is the compromised role played by universities in sustaining rather than acting as the critic and conscience of existing social arrangements. One of the very few vice chancellors to speak out about what might be described as a crisis of legitimacy in higher education is Professor Greg Craven of the Australian Catholic University, who in 2011 commented that Australian universities have been unable to 'articulate a vision of themselves to the public' and that they should be part of a 'constitutional social concept' that enables universities to 'stand as inhibitions to all power, be that media, government or business'. Sadly, the corporatisation of the university sector and its adoption of the commercial ethos have seriously diminished its capacity to play such a role.

Lifting the lid

So concerned had I become about the changed nature of university life – the marketisation, the increasing amounts of bureaucracy and needless regulation and so on – that I decided to do something about it. Adopting the pseudonym 'Joseph Gora' (hello all!), I began writing satirical articles for *Campus Review*, followed by *The Australian*'s 'Higher Education' supplement, *Australian Universities Review* and the *Journal of Higher Education and Management*.

The reactions of academics to these articles told me that I had hit a nerve, and that my experiences were shared around Australia – not that I am the first or last to publicly deride universities, as later chapters will show. What my and others' commentaries share is a concern about the loss of academic status and freedom in Australia's universities, and the fact that these institutions have become so tightly shackled to the imperatives of the global capitalist economy. Along with many others, I happen to believe that tertiary education should be free (in both the financial and existential senses of the word), academics liberated from the petty tyrannies of managerial control and excessive administration, and the academy's bureaucrats consigned to non-intrusive clerical positions elsewhere in the public service.

In highlighting the destructive effects of Whackademia on higher education, this book strikes a polemical rather than academic tone similar to that set by my alter ego. There are no methodological statements, footnotes or appendices, although I do include a section on further reading at the end of the book which outlines some key texts that have influenced my thinking. I have also drawn information from newspaper and journal articles, and books, blogs and other online sources. The most resonant voices of academic discontent, however, came from discussions with friends and colleagues at various city and regional universities. I have talked to current and retired academics, casuals through to emeritus professors, and academics from the arts, humanities, social and natural sciences, and I have learned that there is an astonishing consistency in what these folk choose to complain about.

At the very least, the 60 academics I have consulted were not happy campers; nor did they think that things would improve in the near future. Yet their complaints are also the foundations for change. All believed that things could be a lot better for themselves and for their students, especially if the higher education sector's marriage to the market was annulled, and more freedom and autonomy restored to academics. From what they have had to say, it is possible to pinpoint specific areas in university governance, pedagogy and values that concern academics and which affect their ability to become truly civic-minded teachers and researchers. Students would also benefit from such changes by liberating themselves from the shackles of individual benefit (job readiness, career, income), perhaps rendering them more 'rounded', collectively minded citizens. In short, for many academics the basis of complaint is not about technical change to a compromised system of tertiary education, but a fundamental alteration to the values that underpin that system.

Many also argue – and I agree with them – that despite appearances, neo-liberal universities are becoming increasingly irrelevant in a rapidly changing world. The sector's continued dalliance with economic growth, consumerism and unsustainable means of production may well – if they carry on their present course – consign Australia's universities to irrelevance and total zombification, if they aren't there already. The longer universities insist on being part of the current system of free-market economics, the more likely they are to render themselves marginal to the 'blessed unrest' sweeping the globe.

In addition to recording the views and experiences of a small group of academics, the following discussion contains a fair amount of personal reflection, especially in chapter 1 where I recount my own experiences of university life both here and in Britain. In chapter 2 I move on to discuss how Australian universities have sought to sell their branded products in the marketplace. Chapter 3 addresses what I consider to be a key manifestation of Whackademia – its devotion to self-destructive busy-ness – while chapters 4, 5 and 6 discuss how academics experience teaching, research, and university governance. Chapter 7 highlights how academics have variously positioned themselves in relation to Whackademia, in particular those seeking alternatives to the current system. I conclude by arguing that academics should fight back against the system, seek to open up meaningful intellectual spaces, and not merely rely on abstract critiques and pleas for policy change. In short, I believe that academics can and should continue to do something – or something more – to prevent the further slide into bureaucratised and dumbed-down higher education.

The accounts of academics presented in this book reflect not only some deeply felt objections to the work cultures that operate in universities, but also more general concerns about what universities have become, and in this regard they share a lot in common with the large sections of the general public. You might not agree with what I have proposed in terms of change – I'm not sure I always do! – but at least we might be able to go beyond simple complaint. Most importantly, we might have a long-awaited discussion about the values that underpin higher education and the sorts of qualities required of our graduates if they are to become active, fully informed, and yes, 'rounded' citizens.

1

A tertiary odyssey

During the sixties, universities were full of eccentrics and vibrant ideas.

SENIOR ACADEMIC IN PEACE AND CONFLICT STUDIES, VICTORIA

There has to be something better than what we've got ... I honestly would not encourage my PhD students to work in a university. It would be a dereliction of duty on my part.

PROFESSOR OF POLITICAL SCIENCE
A MAJOR NSW METROPOLITAN UNIVERSITY

My personal odyssey through several universities in England and Australia was made on board a rather leaky vessel. The following account is, however, part of a much broader story about how today's universities have devolved into their current state – and what this means for academics who work in such places. At the very least, my own story reveals that significant changes have swept over the higher education sector both here and overseas, and that many of these changes have made life for many academics generally harder and less rewarding. My story begins in the post-hippy, pre-punk, glam rock days of the early 1970s, when I first pondered the thought of entering the hallowed halls of an English university.

Essex ahoy!

On a gloomy afternoon in late September 1973, I was keenly aware that my life was about to take a significant turn. As I waited outside a battered public telephone in one of Coventry's duller suburbs while my girlfriend phoned for the results of my Advanced-level examinations, the qualifications needed to enter university, I reflected on the consequences of either failure or success. Failure would mean a return to more modest ambitions, perhaps three years at a teacher training or local technical college. Success would augur an exhilarating joyride through the unknown world of higher education. After a few minutes of muffled conversation my girlfriend emerged from the booth to inform me that I had indeed obtained the grades I needed to go to Essex University. After much cavorting, kissing, hugging and the rest we proceeded to the local pub to get uproariously drunk. The next morning, over several cups of coffee and a sore head, I also reflected on the months of revision and high hopes that had at last been realised, and on the world – or at least parts of it – that I was about to leave behind.

As the son of working-class Polish migrants, and after having failed the dreaded 11-plus examination that placed me in a juvenile detention centre masquerading as a secondary school, the best I could hope for was an apprenticeship at one of Coventry's many car factories. Like most of my classmates, I had been subjected to a boot-camp education that was geared towards enslavement on the factory floor. To enforce discipline, pupils were caned ('whacked') on a regular basis, and periodically shunted into assemblies where our headmaster – with the rather misleading surname of Hope – would regale us on the need for good order, discipline and devotion to the Catholic faith.

The less-than-subliminal message from our teachers was that we were brawny and macho, occasionally funny – even lovably quirky – but with one or two exceptions, ultimately thick. Perfect material for the assembly line, we were the 'likely lads' so brilliantly described by Paul Willis in *Learning to Labour.* Our career horizons were rather like those of the working-class kids interviewed for *Seven Up!* – the first of the chronological, fly-on-the-wall documentary series of class aspirations in Britain. These aspirations rarely included anything approaching higher education: university was reserved for the posh end of town. In fact, had anyone cared to ask me, say around 1970, what a university was, I probably would have said it was an abattoir or bank.

But here I was, the first snotty-nosed kid from my latter-day industrial school to go to university. I chose to do – I could never bring myself to say 'read' – a degree in what, on the face of it, sounded rather boring: social studies. However, there was good reason for such a choice. As an aspirant mod in the late 1960s, I had taken a great deal of interest in youth cultures, mainly because I liked the clothes and music, and the chance to meet interesting young women. Stan Cohen, who went on to become an internationally renowned criminologist, was then a senior lecturer at Essex and had written a ground-breaking book about the mod movement called *Folk Devils and Moral Panics.* I was captivated by his eloquent analysis of how mods were demonised by the establishment, and for both narcissistic and intellectual reasons I wanted to know a lot more about young people, culture and identity – especially my own.

Duly enthused, off I went with my battered blue suitcase and brown duffle coat to the University of Essex, home of considerable riotous assembly in 1968 and still something of a leftist hot-house on the outskirts of the former Roman fortress town of Colchester. I was ensconced on the tenth floor of Tawney Tower, one of six hideous residential blocks constructed out of what looked like grey slate brick. With fourteen testosterone-charged young males to each floor, the experience of living in Tawney Tower was always likely to be interesting, and so it proved. There were frequent drug-laden parties, booze-ups, wrecked kitchens and sleepless nights to contend with. Silence was a rarity as the dulcet tones of Bob Dylan, Pink Floyd and Van Morrison could be heard day and night through the thin walls.

Given that my first year did not count towards my final degree, I was handed a license to thrill – nine months of parent-free, unrestrained hedonism and not a little intellectual discovery. In addition to spending considerable amounts of time in the student bar and subsequently recovering from hangovers, I joined the Socialist Workers Party, the Campaign for Real Ale and the highly active Apathy Society. (I was prevented from joining the Anti-Apartheid Group by the Socialist Workers Party because, as I was told by a Frederick Engels lookalike, it was a counter-revolutionary movement.) Obsessed with incoherent ideological questions, I spent many hours bent over the impenetrable – at least to me – works of Marx and Engels, attending long and boring meetings, and trying unsuccessfully to chat up female party-members. On campus, in pubs, common and student rooms, there was always a conversation to be had, an argument to pursue, a position to defend, and a protest to plan. I honed many irritating linguistic skills during this period – not the best asset for someone already infused with considerable arrogance. The student bar and cafeteria were at times the shadow hedonistic equivalent of the Enlightenment's salons, where students of mostly left-leaning political persuasions indulged in visions of a new world order.

In between such encounters I attended lectures delivered by a number of internationally recognised sociologists like Stan Cohen, Dennis Marsden, Peter Townsend (not of The Who), David Lockwood, Joan Busfield, Tony Woodiwiss, Colin Bell, Howard Newby, Ken Plummer, George Kolankiewicz and many others: all outstanding and widely published scholars in their respective fields. I can still recall particular lectures that were brilliantly formulated, interesting, entertaining and insightful – all without the assistance of Power Points, electronic whiteboards and other forms of techno-wizardry. Also absent were on-line lecture notes and lecture streaming, simply because cyber technologies had not yet taken hold in the university system.

The only material we received from our lecturers was a modest subject outline comprising a few yellow, pink or blue pages that included a reading list, essay questions and, if we were lucky, accompanying criteria. No-one spoke of these as 'contracts'. In contrast to today's information overload, there was no chunky, standardised unit information guide written in the parlance of teaching and learning experts, nor did our subject outlines contain complex cross tabulations of graduate attributes, and complex learning objectives. There were no quizzes, multiple choice examinations, or essay questions accompanied by pages and pages of detailed instructive notes. We were largely left to our own devices and used our personal resources, such as they were, to hunt down readings, organise essay material and formulate arguments. There were no consultation sessions with learning support personnel, mentors or peers, since most students who had completed their A-levels had already been well grounded in essay writing.

The teaching staff spent most of their time doing research, scholarship and community service, and most were *bona fide* public intellectuals. Students rarely sought out academics beyond the narrow consultation times. Frankly, we wouldn't have dared, since academics were imbued with god-like qualities, and most students were wary of them. That said, academic staff did hold the occasional party, often at their own homes, and a few of them joined in refectory discussions and student demonstrations. Generally though, academic–student relations were respectful, if a little distant. There were certainly no 'corridor tarts' (students who perpetually hang around academic staff seeking privileged access and, hopefully, better grades) in evidence.

Somehow – spontaneously, miraculously – we managed to produce reasonable essays, to learn independently, and to engage in what was a vibrant, exciting educational process, and all this without any mention of 'excellence', 'innovation', 'creativity', 'opportunity', 'discovery', 'choice' and other such weasel words. Although I spent most of my first year in various states of inebriation and delirium, or in riots and other forms of political activity, I nonetheless managed to learn a great deal through what was an exciting mix of curricular and extra-curricular activities. Eventually I got bored of the failed sex romps and hangovers and decided to get serious about my studies. So, in my second year I moved out of Tawney Tower into more sedate student accommodation about a mile away from the main campus. In hindsight, my first year at Essex could not have been a better learning experience: a combination of formal pedagogy and informal hilarity, political activism, and what gurus of the soul now like to refer to as 'personal growth'. (The other main area of growth – my beer gut – was the product of my very dedicated participation in the Campaign for Real Ale).

After a further two years of publicly funded education – most students got grants in those days and only worked during the summer breaks – I emerged with a head full of wonderful experiences, new interests and fresh insights. Admittedly, the University of Essex was a quirky place, having ridden on the ebbing (though still thrilling) wave of late 1960s radicalism. But the blend of cerebral infusion obtained in refectories, bars, dorms, tutorial rooms and lecture theatres was to provide me with enduring memories and a solid platform for later life. In short, Essex was alive; it had zest and soul. It was an experience similar to Mungo MacCallum's 'getting of ignorance' at St Andrews College at the University of Sydney, where he indulged in the philosophising, carousing, 'dabbling in creativity, exchanging witticisms and partners' that made his university days a 'holistic' and 'special experience'. 'For a brief time', MacCallum remembered, 'we were the chosen ones'. At Essex, I too had known that feeling.

To the Antipodes

In 1977 I made my way to Bristol University in the west of England. Having enrolled in a masters course in race and ethnic relations, I attended regular lectures and tutorials held in a converted Victorian house in the middle of the city. Fortunate enough to have received a scholarship from the Social Science Research Council, I completed coursework and a half-baked thesis on Auguste Comte's ramblings on 'race'. Again, there were few supportive learning props, and we were expected to get on with the task of assignment completion. We received brief subject guides, two days of induction and that was it, we were off and running. Extra-curricular activities included parties at the houses of teaching staff and regular forays into the Edwardian cider houses of Clifton. Later that year, having completed my degree, I headed for York University to embark on a PhD which (like over 40 per cent of students at the time) I never completed, mainly because my scholarship ran out and I found the combination of work and study too much.

After several years as a research officer in probation and social work departments in the Home Counties and London, and a three-year stint in child protection work, in 1991 I moved back into academia with a lectureship in social work at James Cook University in the steamy North Queensland city of Townsville. Located at the foot of Mount Stuart and covered in tropical vegetation, the university offered a pleasant respite from the demands of child protection in cold, soggy inner London. I spent several very happy years at the university, which demanded a great deal in terms of teaching and administration but still allowed me enough time and space to pursue my research and scholarly interests.

In the early 1990s it was still possible to remain relatively autonomous as an academic and to pursue one's scholarly interests without the constant gaze of faculty administrators and quality assurance personnel. The regulatory gaze, such as it was in the department of social work, was minimal and though I'm sure I must have had them, I cannot recall completing a period of probation or other bureaucratic rites of passage. (If they did occur they were mercifully perfunctory.) I also have few recollections of having to complete long and labour-intensive forms for holiday leave or conference attendance, both of which were granted readily and without the rancour, suspicion or spite prevalent in some of today's universities. My performance reviews, such as they were, manifested in occasional casual chats with a kind and attentive head of school, and I never felt any sense of being scrutinised or held to account on 'goal-related activities'.

James Cook's social work department operated largely on good faith, and the majority of academics responded accordingly. There was little or no monitoring of my classes by teaching and learning experts, although we did undertake student evaluations of our units and spoke regularly with student representatives about pedagogical matters, and our unit information guides were subject to informal peer review. Given the good-will that operated in the department, such reflective exercises were conducted in the best spirit of collegial co-operation. Not that everything was always bliss in the department. Occasional conflicts and rivalries arose between academic staff-members, and I witnessed occasional tantrums and tears, but rarely enough to seriously disrupt the day-to-day flow of departmental life. The social work program had been in place for a number of years and we managed to avoid the horrors of repeated restructures. In fact, to this day the school of social work at James Cook University remains one of the most stable and enduring programs in Australia with, by all accounts, a post graduate entry programme that is flourishing. You may wonder why on earth I left such an oasis. The answer? Townsville was too hot, even for a sun worshipper like me.

After a brief stint in 1996–1997 at the University of the Sunshine Coast – then a starchy place run by three male deans and a vice chancellor who liked his trees in neat rows and campus buildings bereft of character – I moved to the School of Justice Studies at the Queensland University of Technology in Brisbane. QUT advertised itself boldly as 'A University for the Real World'. The school, which focused on policing, security, intelligence and various criminal justice issues, was managed by a refugee from the 1960s with a trimmed, greying beard and a protective and assertive instinct that eventually put him out of favour with the university's senior management. For me, however, he was the perfect blend of a left-leaning ideologue, warm, generous and understanding, and wonderfully cynical about the self-evident oddities of the evolving 'enterprise' university – of which QUT was a front-runner. He tried to balance the precarious existence of the school (which was continually under siege from the ambitious law school) with the imperatives of marketised education, especially the need to generate income through increased student enrolments.

I was at the school for eighteen rather pleasant months before the head lost his position to a person who, as far as some of us could tell, had little appreciation of what it meant to be an academic. Despite the fact that several highly accomplished and eminently suitable senior academics had been interviewed for the position, it was the non-academic who landed the job. Problems arose right from the off in terms of concerns about the new head's ability to understand the nuances of academic culture and the particular idiosyncrasies of staff in the school. But none of this seemed to matter to many of my colleagues. The rest of us smouldered with quiet resentment at the injustice of losing a decent head of school with an academic pedigree.

In sanctioning the appointment of the new school head, QUT's senior management had effectively endorsed many of the changes (outlined in the next chapter) that were sweeping over higher education during the 1990s. They argued that the time had come to employ managers from non-academic backgrounds who could take schools and faculties into new corporatised, income-generating directions. At the time, all the talk in school meetings was of the urgent need to increase enrolments, how to keep the student-shoppers satisfied, how to lower attrition rates and haul in large grants. Few if any of my academic colleagues had the courage or wherewithal to question the new corporate orthodoxy. Most simply got on with the job, however excessive the administrative and bureaucratic duties or whatever the ideological rationale behind them. Resistance was confined to occasionally complaining behind closed doors or muttering to oneself. Public complaint appeared to be anathema.

At various times the school was visited by Professor Peter Coaldrake, QUT's then deputy vice chancellor, and since April 2003 its vice chancellor. (Until 2011, he also doubled as the chair of Australian Vice Chancellors' Committee, itself recently re-branded as Universities Australia.) Perhaps not the most loved and admired of people in Queensland – given his past hatchet work while chair of Queensland's Public Sector Management Commission – Coaldrake's vision for QUT has been to create a university of the twenty-first century, where the 'new humanities' are constituted as 'creative industries' that include courses in architecture, visual design, media studies, writing and publishing, advertising and marketing, and creative software applications – definitely not the 'old' humanities!

Not one to mince his words, Coaldrake has repeatedly called for more government funding of higher education and increased philanthropic donations. In his address to the National Press Club in March 2010, he warmly embraced the new culture of quality assurance, and was fully supportive of university performance rankings – although almost as an afterthought, he asserted that we have to 'be very careful in the university system in terms of what you're measuring'. Perhaps most telling in Coaldrake's vision of the contemporary university was the absence of any reference to the lived realities of academic life. He made no mention in his address of the routine complaints, grumbles and discontents of academics as they struggled with the often intolerable demands placed upon them.

Given the above, academic staff in justice studies understandably viewed Coaldrake's visits to the school with considerable suspicion.

Reassurances about the future of our school were greeted with scepticism, and his lengthy homilies on the new realities of higher education were the subject of barely concealed yawns. Our concerns were later increased with news that QUT's Carseldine campus in northern Brisbane was closed, much to the consternation of campus workers and local residents. Staff at the justice studies school were surely justified in feeling a little worried.

My lasting memory of the school is of the overlooked head on his final day, busily packing boxes and removing posters and other ephemera from walls and doors. Before he had time to get out the door, two humourless workmen arrived to remove his name-plate from the door, and replace it with the new nomenclature. Soon afterwards a carton containing expensive red wine arrived for Monday's installation of the new head. As the former head left the building, distant guffaws of laughter could be heard from those academics who had no moral qualms over his departure or concerns about an appointment process that was less than transparent. This was regime change at its ugliest.

Cross purposes

During my five years at QUT, I became increasingly worried by the growing corporatisation of Australian universities. I even organised a conference titled 'Beyond the Enterprise University' which had more speakers than audience members. Eventually, I left QUT in 2002 to take up a senior lectureship at Southern Cross University in the New South Wales coastal town of Coffs Harbour. Given that the red-brick campus had apparently been designed by the same architect who envisioned Grafton Gaol, I should have known better than to depart my metropolitan enclave for what one of my new colleagues referred to as a 'regional gulag'.

SCU had for a brief period in the 1990s gained an enviable reputation as a funky outfit located in Lismore, only a brief drive away from the coastal playground of Byron Bay – now an appallingly overcrowded and expensive parody of its former self. The university had sought to develop new cutting-edge, niche courses like complementary medicine, contemporary music and later, surfing studies. It hoped that such offerings would elevate its image from that of a regional outpost to a bastion of neo-Bohemian excellence, thereby enabling it to attract more students and generate much needed income. For a while it worked, but then the university slipped back into the lower levels of university rankings where it has more or less languished ever since (even though it has a number of outstanding scholars, schools and research centres). Successive vice chancellors struggled to stop the haemorrhaging of students to other universities, but without much success.

While the university continued to be viewed widely as something of a basket case, the new campus at Coffs Harbour held great hope as the way of the future, especially since its tri-sector arrangement with the local TAFE and a senior college was meant to provide a natural flow of students. This experiment at Coffs Harbour was a laudable attempt to develop regional university campuses, but for a variety of reasons – not least that most local students found other universities much more attractive – it eventually failed, and the university was obliged to trawl for students elsewhere, never an easy task in such a ferociously competitive marketplace.

The school which I joined was presided over at various times by heads steeped in micro-management and manifesting significant authoritarian tendencies. Here, unlike James Cook University but not a million miles from QUT, managers were afforded extraordinary powers over academics. Some of my colleagues were encumbered with five years of probation (about the same duration as prison sentences doled out to muggers) and everyone was subject to a highly questionable system of performance review – despite the supposed moderating influence of a very large policy manual. As detailed in later chapters, these reviews – now commonly referred to in the more corporate vernacular as 'performance management development reviews' – were occasionally used to bludgeon academics into submissive conformity or, in my case, to seek revenge for imagined misdemeanours. One person in a senior position had developed a draconian style of management reminiscent of Nurse Ratchet in *One Flew over the Cuckoo's Nest.* Early on I was warned by colleagues to 'keep your head down', 'do as you are told', and 'for God's sake keep under the radar'. This was not unlike my secondary school experience, but without the whack of the cane. Instead, aided by an equally authoritarian colleague, academics were subjected to governance by diktat. It created what one colleague aptly referred to as a 'toxic environment'. The worst treatment was doled out to casuals who, as happens across Whackademia, were subjected to an arbitrary system of governance that occasionally resulted in dismissal without right of appeal. Not surprisingly, droves of good academics left the school to seek renewal elsewhere.

Although this represented an extreme version of the new managerial orthodoxy, it was nonetheless clear that a regulatory regime of top-down domination was abroad in the higher education sector. Granted enormous powers of regulation and control, some managers can now govern as they wish, notwithstanding the 'oversight' (another managerialism blind to its ironic double meaning) of deans, grievance procedures and safeguards contained in policy manuals. These manuals are sometimes used as blunt regulatory instruments, with school heads drawing on obscure sections and sub-sections to demonstrate shortcomings in an academic's performance. I know of one academic who was hounded out of her position after having been repeatedly assailed by a school head for not following policies set out in the policy manual. Academics in my school were vulnerable to such treatment as none had bothered to read the manual – it was enormous, excruciatingly tedious to read and terrifyingly detailed.

During my time at SCU, I became more and more aware not only of the excessive regulation that permeated the university system, but also the strain experienced by students, many of whom sought – and failed – to balance work, family and study. Many external students also felt isolated and marginalised, despite all the talk about 'convergent learning' and endless amounts of 'student support'. Like a lot of other students, they worried about the hefty long-term debts they were incurring under the Higher Education Contribution Scheme.

Yet it was equally clear that over the years students had by default been handed considerable power in Whackademia. End-of-semester student evaluations of teaching performance at SCU were regarded rather like sacred scrolls, as if they possessed the ultimate truths on all matters pedagogical. Despite the fact that such evaluations have largely escaped any meaningful critical scrutiny by their overseers, or recognition that the one-size-fits-all approach produces very limited pedagogical insights, the results of these surveys nonetheless influence everything from academics' performance reviews to promotions.

While personally I was miserable for a lot of my time at SCU, my experience was not necessarily all that different from that of academics in other universities, since the culture of any school or faculty is highly contingent on the personalities involved. I know of many really decent school heads and deans who go out of their way to treat staff with dignity and respect. I am also aware that all heads of school are under great pressure to balance the books and to supervise academic and support staff. This is challenging work, and school heads are ultimately accountable to their deans, and deans to their vice chancellors. That's how the corporate system works.

But this same system – with all its rules and regulations, overarching pressures and competing interests, and top-down governance – also creates the conditions in which overly authoritarian managers can cause havoc. And remember, it's very rare for workers in the corporate system to formally evaluate the performance of their immediate superiors, which makes it difficult to prevent aberrant managerial behaviours.

What made matters even worse for academic staff in my school was the formidable range of routine regulatory practices introduced and overseen by administrative gurus. The most bizarre of these – as many academics will agree – is the workload formula, which was derided by just about everyone subject to it, but treated by management with the reverence it certainly did not deserve. I have a lot more to say about workload formulas in later chapters: for now it is worth noting that as an instrument designed to calibrate work allocation and distribution, the workload formula is of limited usefulness in terms of capturing the everyday realities of academic life.

For academics at SCU, attending to administrative affairs – form filling, preparing reports, completing review documents, applications and so on – largely became the order of the day. Research, at least in my school, was something everyone talked about often but did little about; ditto for writing, and anything approaching public intellectual work. So irrelevant had research become that some academics, with virtually no track record in research and publications but a healthy history of committee attendance, student supervision and administrative labour, were promoted to senior positions. Lack of research among my immediate academic colleagues, however, was more a symptom of system failure. Excessive administrative and teaching duties often squeezed out the time to do research, which for some could only be undertaken during periods of study leave.

That said, academics were required to undertake research as part of their overall duties – and in accordance with the workload formula. Failure to achieve specific goals or to 'perform' adequately in such areas would be met during performance reviews with raised eyebrows, rebukes and/or a re-setting of priorities and goals through 'profiling'. From the standpoint of the academic, such goals were at best a calculated amalgam of minimal aims and intentions that made the daily grind tolerable. Our main tactic to manage these workload calculations was to understate what was achievable, by claiming all sorts of obstacles and impediments, and thus setting the precedent for even more modest targets the following year. Although admirable, honesty and enthusiasm were qualities best tempered during the process of performance review. Over the years I had seen many an eager young permanent academic with his or her nose pressed firmly to the grindstone as a result of having tried to impress a faculty administrator with eagerness to perform multifarious duties. Unscrupulous managers would of course lap up such selfless devotion.

Satisfying the punters

While management practices at SCU offered me a particular insight into the changing nature of university governance, it also shed light on the changing status of students. I became increasingly conscious of the university management's obsession with student enrolment and retention, and the often desperate attempts by academics to ensure student satisfaction. It seemed that managers and academics would do almost anything to keep students rolling through the doors and the cash register turning over. Concerns over income generation appeared to permeate the entire academy. For instance, the intellectual rigour of unit contents was more often than not secondary to the imperative of keeping the punters satisfied – which meant getting them through courses with what amounted to 'soft assessment' and 'soft marking'. Such problems have been widely identified by academic observers, and in the case of Victoria, that state's ombudsman.

At SCU, management directed us to offer all first year students the chance to resubmit failed assignments. We were also encouraged – subtly and otherwise – by deans and school heads, and at board of assessor meetings, to minimise fail grades, and to offer all manner of learning support. Additionally, 'moderation' exercises aimed at ensuring consistency across the student cohort had the effect of minimising fail grades. Noting this problem, a Deakin academic in *The Australian*'s 'Higher Education' supplement of 2 November 2011 remarked: 'So what do you think the majority of academics who don't need to go through the hassles are going to do?' The answer of course is that many simply passed students who in more enlightened times would have failed outright – a practice also noted by many academics interviewed for this book. I once remarked to a colleague that if I were to mark honestly, I would have regularly failed over a third of my students, but such an act would have been greeted with institutional opprobrium – and possibly a please explain from the vice chancellor himself.

The problem at SCU, as elsewhere in Whackademia, is that student support for essay writing and other forms of assessment was limited. At the Coffs Harbour campus, the burden of assisting students with essays fell to one permanently exhausted sessional worker on a recurring contract. Given the significant numbers of overseas students we had to deal with, as well as domestic students who could barely construct a coherent sentence – both the result of the pressure to increase student numbers and revenue – this sort of support proved woefully inadequate.

Consequently, lecturers had to contend with essays written in what may as well have been ancient Greek or pidgin English and without a trace of discernable argument or intellectual coherence. Often, the only bits of essays that made sense were the quotes lifted from textbooks. Given such difficulties and the attempt by many of my colleagues to manage workload pressures, other means of assessment were devised, including the proliferation of multiple choice or take-home examinations and quizzes. Rarely were these attempts at assessing the supposed knowledge of students subjected to the critical scrutiny that they warranted. Instead, education was increasingly reduced to a process of learning-by-numbers, whereby bits of fragmented knowledge were regurgitated via one-liners, ticks and numerical scores.

At the end of each semester the board of assessors – a ritualised forum to review students' marks – agonised over the allocation and distribution of grades, especially the proportion of fails. At SCU, the board also considered how to address the problems of 'at risk' students. (Interestingly, the needs of high-achieving students were usually ignored, which was surprising given the income-generating possibilities of future post graduate students.) Farcical in terms of process and almost entirely bereft of intellectual credibility, these meetings largely ignored pedagogical matters and the intellectual rigour of unit content in favour of rubber-stamping the mediocrity dictated by the bell curve – and quashing any sign of dissent to the whole bizarre procedure.

Despite their many challenges, small regional universities like SCU have demonstrated remarkable resilience over the years. Millions of dollars have been allocated by SCU to build another new campus on a vacant site near Coolangatta airport, the main terminus for tourists visiting the Gold Coast. SCU management remain very excited about this campus's new income-generating possibilities with full-fee-paying students jetting in from China, India and Japan attracted as much by the golden beaches and glitz of Surfers Paradise and the splendour of the adjacent hinterland as they are by a Western education. The campus is also near to one of Australia's most rapidly growing urban centres, its population predicted to increase by over two million over the next couple of decades.

Undeterred by the fact that much of the Gold Coast is at serious risk of floods and inundation as a result of rising sea levels, SCU marketing personnel are champing at the bit to promote surf central to a new student cohort in what will be an enlarged, and from 2012, fully deregulated market. The university will of course do everything in its power to smooth the entry of students into degree programmes by offering generous credits (already up to 50 per cent), learning assistance and two-year, rapid-fire course completion. Like other campuses around Australia, the new SCU campus will no doubt eventually include cafes, eateries, boutiques, hi-tech sports facilities, specialty stores and counselling services that will accommodate every need of the student-shopper. It may even seek to foster 'interactive community' and 'student engagement' through initiatives already adopted by other universities: cafe-style lecture theatres, electronic communication boards, ergonomically designed park benches, 'village' student accommodation, and comfy study spaces.

Whether or not any of this fosters education, or creates soul or civic purpose is of course another matter entirely. Perhaps that is why, in a May 2010 article in the *Sydney Morning Herald* – drawing on recent research carried out by the Centre for the Study of Higher Education at the University of Melbourne, the National Union of Students and the Griffith Institute for Higher Education – Heath Gilmore was able to comment so negatively about the modern experience of being a university student:

> Students are treating university like an intellectual fast-food restaurant, and academics are being left to assume a new role as mere drive-through classroom attendants ... Super-organised and technologically wired but time-poor, modern students regard university as another appointment on their electronic organiser, new research shows ... They drop into the required lecture or tutorial and fill up on the required amount of education before motoring on to their part-time job, one eye on the Higher Education Contribution Scheme debt they are racking up.

As 'drive-through classroom attendants', academics might well feel that their work has been reduced to the menial task of serving up what the consumer wants, irrespective of the ultimate effects on all concerned. The main objective is to keep the student-shoppers rolling through the doors.

I will argue later that in the short to medium term, academics might seek to develop practices that promote aspects of university education that are grounded in the intrinsic worth of learning and the goals of active citizenship and civic engagement. Instead of mindlessly embodying a productivist logic, universities might reflect on how we can produce graduates who are imbued with wisdom, kindness, compassion and an understanding of peace, citizenship, rights, social justice and sustainability. But I'm afraid you won't see many references to such matters in university mission statements or advertising slogans, which I consider in the next chapter.

2

Sexing up Whackademia

You can understand why so much money is spent on marketing. It has become part of the organisational culture, and the taken-for-granted objective of increasing participation without adequate levels of funding.

SENIOR LECTURER IN SOCIAL WORK, VICTORIA

Sometimes it feels as if we're all working in a supermarket.

SENIOR LECTURER IN ARTS, ADELAIDE

Universities are all about the brand, mate.

LECTURER IN JUSTICE STUDIES, BRISBANE

Despite all the marketing and public relations exercises, and talk of the 'academic citizen' and the 'republic of learning', Australian universities remain rather insular places. While not exactly sealed institutions like prisons, asylums or monasteries – although some academics might even argue this point – universities often appear cut off from the outside world: hence the repeated existential shocks that occur when academics venture beyond their campuses only to find that few if any of their thoughts matter a jot to the local butcher, baker or hairdresser. Universities like to claim they are an integral part of their local communities. They even appoint people responsible for 'community engagement', although this is more often than not a by-word for a commercial dalliance with local business, or a handy partnership for a grant application. In practical terms, however, most universities have only a passing acquaintance with the local citizenry.

Occasionally academics do venture beyond university precincts and may sit on boards, inquiries and management committees, offer their advice to industry, present papers at conferences, act as advocates and give occasional media interviews. However, for many academics 'community service' may not even figure as part of their workload calculations. (This was certainly the case at my last university, where my school head seemed to view community service as irrelevant to the main task of teaching.) On most workdays – which for those frantically labouring to satisfy their workload formulae usually means seven days a week – academics can be found in their office-cells glued to computer screens or at home in the same sort of taxing ergonomic posture.

Most university campuses are rather dull places, especially during the holiday season when they are invariably devoid of significant human presence. Campuses do, however, come to life during the semester, mainly because students and academics are hanging around and there are boutiques, bars, cafes and brasseries to frequent, resplendent fountains and gardens to visit, libraries to trawl through, and lectures and tutorials to attend.

On a good day visitors interested in university campuses might choose to survey the Oxbridge-like sandstone buildings at the universities of Sydney, Melbourne, Queensland or Adelaide – they at least look like the real thing – or the splendid Japanese gardens at the University of Southern Queensland. But it is hard to imagine tourists like Fred and Doris from Cornwall or Heinz and Boris from Berlin travelling half-way round the world to visit the Wagga Wagga campus of Charles Sturt University, or the University of Central Queensland in beef-producing Rockhampton. Equally, any thrill-seeking American tourists would surely not travel to Australia simply to view RMIT's modernist monoliths, the tower blocks at UTS in central Sydney, or the solitary daffodil-yellow edifice at the new Southern Cross University campus on the Gold Coast.

Universities, however, have long figured in the Australian cultural landscape, and the nation currently boasts 39 of them. That's about one for every half a million people, which, according to Professor Peter Coaldrake, is just about right. Notwithstanding the fact that there are in the order of 150 private colleges that also provide higher education services – although some of them with suspect pedigrees – as well as some TAFE colleges and overseas institutions trying to get in on the act, universities remain the main providers in the field. And of course there are nowadays a lot more students to deal with. According to the Department of Employment, Training and Workplace Relations, the student population numbered around in 485 000 in 1990, about 695 000 in 2000 and rose to well over a million in 2010, including some 57 000 post-graduate students. Quite how we got to these sorts of figures is a story to which we now turn.

Making universities pay

Thanks in part to what Simon Marginson and Mark Considine describe as the 'win and crush' tactics of the former Labor Minister of Employment, Education and Training, John Dawkins, we now have a system of higher education that resembles a collection of factories tailored to the productive requirements of Australia's globalised economy. For Marginson and Considine, Dawkins was 'the model neo-liberal executive, forcing through a single-minded reform crusade with a mix of system planning, market rhetoric, and the determination to crush all political opposition'. Faced with what he and his neo-liberal acolytes considered to be an outdated and elitist system of higher education that was over-reliant on the public purse, in 1987 Dawkins set about revolutionising the tertiary sector.

The Dawkins plan for an expanded, market-based system of higher education was set out initially in a Green Paper, *Higher Education: A Policy Discussion Paper*, and a year later in *Higher Education: A Policy Statement*. (The startling similarities between these documents tended to suggest that the consultation processes were somewhat less than comprehensive.) Nonetheless, key to Dawkins' proposals was the upgrading and merging of universities with various colleges of advanced education and other education institutions. To offset the budgetary pressures that were likely to result from this expansionary exercise, Dawkins proposed that universities should develop a mixed system of public and private funding, student co-payments and encourage full-fee paying student enrolments from Asia and elsewhere.

Integral to his vision of a self-regulated university system grounded in the global economy – a vision no doubt inspired by free-market luminaries like Milton Friedman, Margaret Thatcher and Ronald Reagan – Dawkins asserted that universities should adopt the fundamentals of the business model. This meant embracing 'entrepreneurship' and the practices of setting targets, developing market plans and introducing performance controls: the same organisational approach that had already been widely adopted across industrial sectors in a number of other Western countries. Essentially, Dawkins viewed universities as centres of industrial production vital to Australia's economic and therefore national interests. According to Marginson and Considine, Dawkins held a 'productivist concept of value' that enabled him to reconfigure the day-to-day operations of universities along strictly economic fundamentalist lines, resulting in the rapid growth of student enrolments in a hugely competitive higher education sector. Inevitably, class sizes mushroomed and academics pressured to work harder – despite the fact that they were struggling to make sense of a system that was subject to constant change, reinvention and shifting goal posts.

Not surprisingly, as the years rolled by academics found it difficult, if not impossible, to adapt to the new order, even more so when the student-shopper was gradually elevated to god-like status and invited to put into practice the neo-liberal mantras of freedom of choice and flexibility. From the early 1990s onwards, academics found themselves confronted by a number of discomforting developments: reduced government funding (which eventually led Universities Australia in 2010 to plead for $881 million of additional funding or face a risk to 'quality and/or sustainability'); increased student numbers; and the emergence of a more powerful hierarchy of administrators and heads of school.

Consequently, the status of academics declined rapidly, and the more that universities expanded their commercial activities the less managers and administrators took seriously the interests of academics. As Marginson and Considine observed in 2000, 'academic sensibilities are having a diminishing influence on the development of universities, those who argue that universities should be treated as just another business are getting their way, and the university imagination is increasingly a managerial imagination'. This was really a polite way of saying that academics were being screwed over by bosses whose primary interest was, and remains, the bottom line.

The bottom line of course was part of a larger project designed, as Marginson and Considine put it, 'to advance the prestige and competitiveness of the university as an end in itself'. Post-Dawkins universities found themselves in increasingly cut-throat competition with each other and with universities overseas that were themselves undergoing similar ideologically driven changes. They were all vying for student enrolments, grants and the ever-diminishing trough of government funding. The 'sandstone' universities like Sydney, Melbourne, Tasmania and Queensland – established in the state capitals before World War I – continued to do rather well in the open market, but the 'gumtree' universities established in the 1960s and 1970s, like James Cook, Griffith and Newcastle, and the 'new' universities, like Canberra, Edith Cowan and Notre Dame, struggled for a decent slice of the pie.

It was in such relatively impoverished places that the loudest tin-rattling could be heard, as university managers desperately sought to shore up student numbers in order to balance the books. In the shark-infested waters of marketised tertiary education, the brand became everything. Each university sought to appear as if it were offering a superior quality product compared to its competitors. Universities felt compelled to portray themselves as bastions of excellence, creativity, innovation, opportunity and choice; friendly, fun-filled places with endless support, flexible course offerings and all manner of frolics and edu-tainment. Most importantly, universities lured potential students by selling the idea that higher education was the fast-lane to the profitable professional career of their choice.

To this end, courses were tailored to meet the interests and aspirations of both prospective students and employers. In effect this meant that the role of the lecturer was increasingly reduced to that of a process facilitator – someone whose primary duty is to ensure that students get through their courses and into the professional workforce as smoothly as possible.

Selling the university brand to a mass audience was by no means an easy task, so our non-sandstone desperados went on the offensive by pumping tens of millions of dollars into the creation and expansion of their marketing, promotions, communication and public relations departments. Soon, a new cadre of high-paid personnel steeped in psycho-social marketing babble took hold of the reins in order to sell their competing brands to a growing market of potential students-shoppers both here and overseas. Today, the wonders of university education are marketed, unabashedly and with great vigour and purpose, through TV commercials, newspaper supplements and advertisements, cinema advertising, on the sides of buses and taxis, and on giant billboards at railway stations and shopping malls. University degrees are generally viewed by marketing personnel as commodities to be sold to consumers, just like cornflakes, baked beans, designer shoes and whisky-flavoured condoms.

Furthermore, rather than simply seeking to maximise profits, universities have sought to generate sufficient funds to plug the fiscal gap created by years of inadequate government funding. In fact, this was the key intention of Dawkins' reforms. As Marko Beljac neatly puts it, those reforms aimed 'to embrace the market and to socialise profit-seeking'. All that this line of logic requires is that the public relations folk devise ways of persuading the prospective student of the education-product's superior quality and distinctiveness: the rest should follow. University products – like degrees, diplomas, certificates and doctorates – are sold to anyone who is remotely eligible, which, thanks to relaxed entry requirements, now includes most of the adult population.

In addition to generating funds through student enrolments, universities also invite contributions from alumni and private companies. Many universities advertise their sponsors, and all put out regular calls for tax-deductible 'corporate sponsorship/support', the fruits of which find their way to funding research initiatives, sporting activities, prizes, conferences, scholarships, exchange programs and student industry placements. Dozens of professorial positions are also sponsored by private corporations. For instance, a *Sydney Morning Herald* survey in 2007 identified several sponsored professorial positions, like the National Australia Bank professor of finance at the University of Sydney, the Pfizer chair of clinical pharmacy and the Microsoft chair of innovation at Macquarie University, and the Multiplex chair of engineering construction innovation at the University of NSW. More recently, in 2010, four separate chairs in mining and energy research at the University of Western Australia were sponsored by companies such as Chevron, Woodside and Alcoa.

The list of sponsors or 'mutually beneficial partnerships' linked to universities is breathtaking and includes literally hundreds of contributors like state and federal government, banks, insurance companies, multinational mining and energy companies, media corporations and umpteen local businesses. By contributing to a gold, platinum or bronze sponsorship or via a simple donation, companies can – according to the gushing blurb on university websites – enhance brand awareness among student populations and offer them a route straight into the corporate world via scholarships and industry placements. In effect, such sponsorships and donations are, as noted over a decade ago by Naomi Klein in *No Logo*, a major source of brand advertising for companies in the education sector: a source that also carries with it the potential for conflicts of interest, undue influence on curriculum content, and negative public perceptions.

But the most feverish commercial activity in today's university system is the peddling of products to prospective students. This is considered 'bread and butter' activity pivotal to the survival of each institution. All 39 universities promote their wares on the open market using every conceivable marketing trick in the book. The 'sexing up' of Whackademia – an awful necessity occasioned by years of government underfunding and the imposition of free-market ideology – has led to a bizarre world of commercial gimmickry and puerile pyrotechnics in which slogans, mottos and other expressions of the corporate imagination have largely replaced substance. I turn my attention here to just a few examples of such oddities in the hope that this will reveal how far universities have become compromised in the new reality.

Image-building

Australian universities have long sought to promote themselves in the public eye and to present themselves as centres of higher order learning, scholarship and groundbreaking research. Mottos – symbolic phrases and insignia denoting lofty principles or ideals – have traditionally played a key role in conveying an impression of historical longevity, anchored in an institutional lineage that can be traced to the earliest days of Oxford and Cambridge or even to ancient Greece. Fifty years ago, these cultural symbols were more concerned with demonstrating an intellectual pedigree rather than propping up the market ambitions of their respective universities. Mottos are now part of a great panoply of mass marketing tag-lines that focus on bolstering market position rather than celebrating the intrinsic virtues of learning.

The quaint yet antiquated use of Latin phraseology often contained in mottos seems somewhat at odds with the modern hard-nosed approach taken by corporate marketing departments in today's universities. Nonetheless, universities seem to have retained mottos because they feel there is market value in such symbols – perhaps even because they genuinely believe that the 'republic of learning' has its roots in a less commercialised era. Not surprisingly, mottos continue to exude great scholastic seriousness. Take the following examples:

- ANU: '*Naturam primum cognoscere rerum*' (First, [let him busy himself] to learn the nature of things)'
- Monash: '*Ancora imparo*' (I am still learning)
- RMIT: '*Perita manus mens exculta*' (Skilled hands and cultured minds)
- New England: '*Veritatis studium prosequi*' (To pursue the study of truth)'
- Melbourne: '*Postera crescam laude*' (We grow in the esteem of future generations)
- UNSW: '*Manu et mente*' ([Knowledge by] hand and mind)
- Southern Queensland: '*Per studia mens nova*' (Through study the mind is transformed)
- Sydney: '*Sidere mens eadem mutato*' (The constellation is changed but the disposition is the same).

As noted, mottos are only one part of the great flow of corporate marketing emissions that aspire to other-worldly elitism. These include mission/vision/value statements which vary wildly in both tone and content but which seek to fulfil the same aim: namely, to convey the nuanced and potent mythology of each institution. Consider, for instance, the following statement from La Trobe University: 'La Trobe University will continue to enhance its profile nationally and internationally and will achieve wide recognition for delivering socially responsible, inclusive, relevant and radical learning, teaching and research'. Quite what 'radical learning' means in the context of today's higher education system is hard to fathom, but there's no doubting La Trobe's commitment to positioning itself via the usual mantras as a robust higher education institution in the global marketplace. Few doubts also linger around Macquarie University's blunderbuss vision statement:

> To establish a pervasive research culture across all areas of the University, and to achieve internationally and nationally leading research in selected concentrations of research excellence, by maximising the institution's intellectual and physical resources and by maintaining a continuous improvement framework.

Although forthright and outspoken – as well as full of weasel words – Macquarie's statement provides little indication of the values that underpin its energetic intentions.

Less forceful in tone is UNSW's pitch: 'By providing an excellent educational experience and by achieving excellence in research, international engagement and interaction with the community UNSW will be an international university of outstanding quality'. At least the University of Southern Queensland makes an attempt to sketch in some details about what it hopes to achieve. 'Our mission', declares its website 'is to enable broad participation in higher education and to make significant contributions to research and community development'. This will be supposedly achieved through maintaining USQ as a viable enterprise that:

- offers quality professional education opportunities that are accessible, flexible and borderless

- creates fulfilling experiences for all students based on the commitment of skilled and caring staff
- develops graduates who are positioned to meet the challenges of a rapidly changing world
- pursues world-class research, innovation and practice in sustainable futures
- engages with communities, business and government through ongoing and mutually beneficial partnerships.

But what if I happen to reject the invitation to join the globalised, corporate, flexible, innovative and borderless world (if, in fact, such a world exists)? Maybe I could apply to another university, but then again, they all seem to make the same sort of siren call. Perhaps that's the point about all these clichéd statements: they take it for granted that students want to or should become embedded in a world of enterprise and productivist logic that feeds into a corporatised, capitalist world. Maybe that's why all these value/mission statements sound so dreadfully similar and are entirely incapable of imagining an alternative way of being.

Slogfest

If mottos and vision/mission statements are the staid commercial outpourings of the corporate university, slogans are their simple 'Oi! Oi! Oi!' With the help of the internet, TV, cinema and newspaper advertising, university slogans are positioned slap-bang in the middle of a very public domain. They are plastered on websites, letterheads, envelopes, hoardings, T-shirts, football socks, shorts, coffee mugs, key rings and business cards. They are meant to convey character, distinctiveness and quality that sets one university apart from its competitors. And this is where the marketing personnel, public relations experts, media specialists and 'community engagement officers' come in. It is their brief to create the technologies to beguile, seduce and persuade student-shoppers to enrol at their respective institutions – and what better way than a funky slogan! Carefully and skillfully composed, a slogan, if repeated often enough, can gradually form the mental image required to persuade any doubting Thomas that the University of Bleep is well ahead of its rivals – even if it isn't.

Slogans, of course, have also been around for a long time, but since the early 1990s they have become the marketing weapons of choice in Whackademia. There are hundreds of them out there, all seeking to ensnare the potentially lucrative student-shopper. And what a peculiar selection of promotional messages they are, ranging from the crass and inane to the absurd and idiotic. Take the University of Sydney which through its Brand Unit in the Provost's Office has conjured the slogan 'Our people make a difference'. Quite how this is achieved is of course open to speculation, although there is such confidence in this simple but forthright statement that it finds its way into many aspects of the university's promotional material. Sydney's vacuous sloganeering is echoed in countless other institutional emissions, like those from the University of New England in regional New South Wales – 'The UNE experience stays with you for life'; James Cook University's evocation – 'Light ever increasing'; the ANU – 'The truth shall set you free'; or the Australian Catholic University – 'Caring for the world'. Other universities have sought to peddle more punchy slogans that would hopefully find their way deep into the recesses of the potential student-shopper's mind: 'Your global passport' (RMIT); 'Achieving international excellence' (UWA); and 'A university for the real world' (QUT). Somewhat more avuncular in tone is the University of Central Queensland's slogan – 'Be what you want to be' – while the University of Adelaide goes for the short but bold 'Life impact' and UTS for the instructive 'Think, change, do'.

But there was another sort of slogan that smacks of institutional self-righteousness, and which also hugely over-emphasises the influence of universities in everyday life. Examples of such offerings are 'Bringing ambition to life' (Bond University); 'Break out of your comfort zone' (Charles Darwin University); 'The world is your campus' (Monash University); and most starkly, 'Your uni, your life' (University of the Sunshine Coast). Always eager to claim product superiority over its rivals, Southern Cross University's slogan reads: 'A new way to think' – a meaningless edict that led one student to replace the word 'think' with 'stink' on an SCU poster. But surely the prize for the appealing slogan must go to La Trobe University: 'Infinite possibilities to expand your mind'. This beguiling declaration would surely have got the thumbs up from famed exponent of mind-altering substances, Tim Leary, and might have even persuaded Keith Richards to consider hanging out on a Melbourne campus.

Perhaps the most business-like slogans are those that most consistently employ the weasel words of neo-liberal corporate-speak. Aimed at creating the impression of serious scholarship and industrial relevance, these slogans have the air of modernist tedium about them. Cleary the intention of the following staccato phrases is to send certain images racing through the collective psyche of prospective students in the hope of instilling some sort of lasting semiotic effect: 'Progressive, Relevant, Innovative, Responsive' (Deakin University); 'Integrity, Respect, Rational Enquiry, Personal Excellence' (Edith Cowan University); 'In the pursuit of excellence in teaching and research' (Griffith University); and 'Excellence, Innovation, Diversity' (University of Wollongong).

These sorts of sombre, cringe-inducing shibboleths contrast markedly with the more modest but no less universal claims made in the following slogans: 'For the public good' (Charles Sturt University); 'A new school of thought' (Victoria University); 'Inspiring achievement' (Flinders University); and 'Building the foundations for a better future' (University of New South Wales). More pronounced and confident than such offerings are the slogans of the University of Queensland, 'The University of Smart Moves'; the University of South Australia, 'The University of going further'; and, perhaps with one eye on its neighbour, the University of Canberra's 'Australia's Capital University'.

There is of course no necessary connection between what is claimed in such slogans and what actually goes on in universities. In fact, that's the whole point. The purpose of these emissions is to create an impression that covers over the yawning gap between what is claimed by the likes of Universities Australia and what transpires on university campuses.

In some quarters, the above marketing devices are regarded as akin to clumsy acts of seduction. It comes as no surprise therefore to learn that one astute academic observer of the university marketing scene, Arthur O'Neil, has referred colourfully to sloganeering as 'ejaculations'. O'Neil sees these particular corporate emissions as promotional 'come-ons' made up of catchphrases aimed at capturing the interest of readers. He also refers to 'tags' as those trade markers or signs which denote the apparent distinctiveness of particular brands. In his analysis of advertisements placed in various newspapers by Australian universities during a two-month period in 2009 – mostly concerning course offerings and job vacancies – O'Neil lays bare (as it were) the full ephemeral nonsense of the brand-obsessed university culture:

- 'Aim High' and 'Out to achieve' (University of Newcastle)
- 'Rewarding excellence' (Griffith University)

- 'Internationally Renowned' (University of Tasmania)
- 'innovation, diversity & excellence' (University of Wollongong)
- 'Experience the Difference' (University of South Australia)
- 'inspiring achievement' (Flinders University).

And so it goes, on and on.

These tags and ejaculations say everything and nothing about the value of higher education products, since their intent is not to inform but to persuade through the most reductivist use of marketing techniques and the corporate imagination. But do they persuade or irritate readers? O'Neil thinks it is the latter: 'Where universities are concerned, these self-promoting devices often affront the sensibilities of readers. Universities would be better advised to stick to plain announcements and not to debase their worth by decorating them with sales ploys.' Also worrying for O'Neil is that university tags and ejaculations are less than useful in terms of telling us what these institutions actually do:

> That the academy sells itself in the same way as firms spruiking for trade is wonder enough; but that the tags employed, and some of the ejaculations, are so ill-fitted to the purpose, are either silly self-aggrandisements or shallow inducements, demands explanation. What is going on?

Good question! We'll come back to that one.

Web-speak

The most elaborate of all university ejaculations are to be found on the pages of their websites. It's here that folk in corporate communications and marketing departments deploy symbolic images and representations of their respective institutions to an expectant world. And what revealing imaginings they are. After all, websites are windows to the world, a constituent element in the architecture of mass communication, and therefore a vital means of selling the hallowed university brand.

University websites vary enormously in terms of the information and messages that they choose to display. Amid the routine information – like how to enrol, or information on faculties and schools, student services, staff, links, contacts and general whereabouts – are the hooks calculated to lure prospective student-shoppers. Invariably university websites are plastered with hi-definition coloured photographs of youthful student-shoppers in varying states of bliss, as evidenced through the omnipresence of bright eyes, perky postures and pearly white teeth. The occasional 'mature aged' student might make an appearance, and every effort is made to present the multicultural nature of the student population by including a few non-white faces, but the prevailing impression remains one of youthful exuberance set against the vibrant backcloth of parks, tree-lined piazzas, high-tech libraries and trendy cafes and restaurants.

What these pages don't show is equally telling. There's no sign here of students clearing off for the afternoon shift or weighed down by their HECS debt, or of students living in over-crowded, crappy accommodation or struggling to balance family commitments and work – all familiar complaints of real as opposed to virtual students. There is no sign either of the growing evidence of mental health problems among the student body, brought on in part by these unacknowledged pressures. Website campuses are always happy, jovial, exceedingly vibrant and colourful places; perfect for the would-be student-shopper and aficionados of sports facilities and gastronomic outlets.

Academics are also generally conspicuous by their absence from university websites. Very occasionally they are pictured peering over the shoulders of students in laboratories, perhaps scrutinising essays or delivering interactive lectures to transfixed student audiences. More often than not though, it's vice chancellors whose professional portraits appear on university websites, invariably accompanied by a 'welcome' of carefully scripted promotional material. For instance Professor Barney Glover, vice chancellor of Charles Darwin University (CDU), does a terrific job in highlighting what his university has to offer.

CDU, asserts Professor Glover, 'has all of the advantages of a relatively young multi-sector university, including vigour, creativity, flexibility and freedom from the constraints of tradition'. The public renunciation of 'tradition' is rather unusual for a vice chancellor, but Professor Glover clearly considers CDU to be at the upper end of the evolutionary scale. He assures us that instead of tradition:

> the true character and richness [of CDU] stems from its location in the Northern Territory of Australia, centred in Darwin: a youthful, multicultural, cosmopolitan, and robust, tropical city in a Territory that is steeped in Aboriginal tradition and culture and which enjoys a close interaction with the peoples of Southeast Asia.

Professor Glover's pitch for global connectivity is evidenced in the links he draws with other tropical environments and culturally diverse populations. He insists that the diminutive size of CDU is an asset rather than liability: it 'has created a university that is collegial, friendly and confident of its future as a leader in its chosen fields of expertise and also as an institution that provides high quality teaching and services'. If I were looking for a job in Nirvana I might, on the basis of Professor Glover's claims, apply for a job at CDU. But, as an acquaintance who works at the university told me: 'It's about the same as most other universities I have worked in: tremendous amounts of hard work, lots of oversight, bitching and back-biting'.

Persuasive though CDU's website might be in terms of luring prospective student-shoppers, it pales into insignificance when compared to the barrage of propaganda unleashed by some of our sandstone universities. The websites of many of this select club overflow with intoxicating froth and lofty, self-obsessed claims of indefatigable excellence. After all, these are institutions of 'global importance' that put most of our regional universities to shame.

As you might expect, the University of Melbourne has a website that demands attention. Its hard-sell to prospective student-shoppers is an exercise in corporate seduction the likes of which Charles Sturt University and the University of Central Queensland can only dream about. First, the website talks about the university's location – right next to the CBD where there is easy access to cafes, restaurants, shopping centres and major sporting venues. And if you want to know how good all that is then click on the link below and hey presto, there are students raving about the area's attractions. What's more, there are plenty of halls of residence near social central where you can bunker down for a semester or two and party to your heart's content or make use of top-flight sporting facilities. In other words, everything the true hedonist and aspiring professional might wish for.

But there's more, lots more. As a student there are many social and other clubs you can join. There are even 'social justice' clubs and you can 'indulge your passion for chocolate, cooking, Star Trek or debating'. But the coup de grace is Union House on the Parkville campus, which we're told houses cafes, eateries, support services and various retail outlets – no need to wander off to Westfield, it's all here! The night life is something to behold. 'There's always something happening on campus. Any night of the week will see a range of activities on offer: theatre, exhibitions, gigs, trivia nights, comedy and film as well as public lectures. There really is something for all.' If that isn't enough to pull in a few thousand overseas students, I don't know what will.

Considerable space is also devoted to praising the 'Melbourne model', a truncated undergraduate offering that covers six broad areas of study linked to career-oriented postgraduate programmes – though of course there's no mention that the introduction of this model led to the decimation of countless well-established courses and generated student protests and academic layoffs. Rather, it asserts that not only will students be given one of the greatest educational experiences on the planet and prepare them for lucrative professional careers, but along the way they can make use of all the technical armoury and contemporary spatial design at Melbourne's disposal:

> eLearning studios are designed for collaborative work in small groups and have PCs, laptop interconnectivity and data projectors; eSeminar rooms are designed for seminars and presentations that use a range of different media; iMedia theatres and theatrettes have 'lecture capture' that records audio and visual content from lectures making streamed and downloadable versions of these recordings (very handy for those days when you're unavoidably detained or unable to make it on to campus).

Who falls for this sort of techno-erotica? Perhaps it's meant to appeal to the tech-heads – so long as they're not insulted by the assumption that they'll be more impressed by gadgets than actual intellectual content.

Melbourne has yet to create virtual lecturers and seminars, but I'm sure that day will come. Professor Jim Barber, vice chancellor of the University of New England, has already suggested that we should abandon physical campuses and instead engage with each other solely (and soullessly) in cyberspace. Likewise former ALP cabinet minister, Lindsay Tanner, has warned universities that if they fail to adapt to the challenge of global digital technology 'the universities of tomorrow may not be a university at all'. Neither Barber nor Tanner seem to entertain the idea that, as a number of studies show, on-line students often feel isolated and would much prefer direct engagement with others in the process of learning. Nor do they seem to recognise the irony that, by immersing universities in cyberspace and mimicking every other higher education institution on the planet, they may well sow the seeds of their own destruction. After all, isn't 'difference' and 'choice' the great appeal of the modern university? Would some universities not be more distinctive if they guaranteed direct student engagement, a sense of real community and collegiality, and a chance to learn from the wonders of casual social encounters? Perhaps that's what all the cafes are for.

No such grandiose claims are made by the ever-humble University of Notre Dame. Perhaps cognisant that pride is one of the seven deadly sins, it posts the following almost apologetic invitation on its website: '2011 has seen the University of Notre Dame Australia celebrate receiving 5 Stars in 5 Categories for 5 Years in a national survey which benchmarks a standard of excellence in universities and private colleges across Australia'. The rest of its website isn't worth writing about. Nor for that matter are the utterances of Professor Parker on the website of the University of Canberra. His soft-sell to prospective students is about as appealing as last week's rice pudding: 'At the University of Canberra', he intones, 'our focus is on preparing you for a successful and rewarding career. We call it professional preparation for professional careers. And it works.' Professor Parker presumably sees nothing wrong with the idea that a university simply stamps a student's passport to a business career. Pity the bright spark who wants an education, not a qualification.

No such qualms bother testosterone-charged QUT either. Home to three educational 'precincts', QUT boasts on its website a very intimate connection with industry: 'We're well known as "a university for the real world" because of our close links with industry and our relevant teaching and applied research'. The 'real world' then is one that engages the concerns of industry and, by implication, all other airy-fairy aspirants can pursue their ethereal interests – like arts and humanities – elsewhere. The blurb on QUT's website is reminiscent of that peddled by Britain's polytechnics before they were amalgamated into an increasingly bloated university system. The tone is dry, bordering on the dour with more than a hint of self-righteousness. Get real or get lost, the website promo-speak seems to be saying.

Defending the brand

Whatever else they might claim, university websites are technologies of persuasion designed to sell branded products to student-shoppers who are the financial life-blood of every institution. But there is a more sinister side to the sexing up of Whackademia. Given the importance of the brand and all the investment that goes into creating it, university managers can be ever-so-slightly sensitive about any threat to the corporate image, especially if this jeopardises the university's public profile and therefore its ability to attract student-shoppers.

So, the brand has to be protected, and one way of doing this is to ensure that academics are prevented from speaking out on anything beyond their immediate area of 'expertise' and 'specialisation'. In effect, this means that academics are, and have been, significantly constrained from publicly addressing a wide range of issues. The main mechanisms for such regulatory control have been codes of conduct, along with various strictures and coded warnings buried in policy and procedure manuals.

Writing in *The Australian* in 2008, education researchers David Rowe and Kylie Brass analysed ten universities that over the previous six years had adopted policies relating to academics making media comment. Most of these universities had, say the authors, 'bolstered their public comment and/or academic freedom provisions with a view to placing boundaries around the subjects that academics are allowed to discuss in public'. This was achieved by formally prohibiting public comments that seemed to conflict with organisational matters that were the concern of higher university officers, comments that might appear to reflect official university views, or comments that compromised collegial relations within the university. In other words, academics couldn't say anything that might upset the university, its sacrosanct administrators, or other academics. Breaking these rules could be regarded as acts of serious professional misconduct, subject to disciplinary processes orchestrated through performance management reviews or the scrupulous attentions of human relations personnel.

The purpose of such measures, say Rowe and Brass, was to 'prohibit any activity or commentary that, in the terminology of their media policies, "de-position" them; that is, threaten to reduce their standing in the formal and informal rankings that obsess the producers and consumers of 21st century education'. Over the years, the actions taken by universities against those academics who have spoken publicly on issues either within or beyond their designated professional remit suggests an acute sensitivity among managers in our higher education sector. Brand damage can of course have serious implications for today's universities and this explains why more draconian regulatory policies have been applied to today's academics.

As noted by Rowe and Brass: 'greater concern about corporate profile has meant that universities are acutely sensitive to the association between the organisation itself and the public comments of its academics'.

In short, the creation of the university brand and attempts to protect it have come at a very high price in terms of academic freedom. But the glossy outpourings of marketing departments can only disguise so much. Indeed, distorted impressions peddled by these departments are not the only problem here. There's the small matter of cost. As a blogger in *The Age*, Erica Cervini, points out: 'At a time when universities are crying poor, they're spending millions on lame and silly marketing'. But that's what the commercialisation of higher education is all about. It forces institutions into cut-throat competition where brand distinctiveness is pivotal to institutional survival. Without the lurid vacuity of mottos, slogans, tag-lines and web-speak, universities may have to rely on their academic reputations. Some might get away with this, others would simply fold. In the next chapter I begin to lift the lid on everyday university life as experienced by many of today's academics. It's not a pretty picture.

3

Taking care of busyness

Most days I haven't got time to scratch my arse. There's enough administrative stuff to keep us busy all day, but on top of that we have to prepare for and do teaching, put in grant applications, do research, apply for promotion, study leave, attend meetings and do anything else that is required. Fun, eh?

HUMANITIES ACADEMIC, QUEENSLAND

Most days are lousy days. It didn't used to be like that. Sure there are some highlights, like getting things published or obtaining a grant, but the daily toil of trying to get on top of all the bureaucratic demands is exhausting.

AN INTERNATIONALLY RENOWNED PROFESSOR IN THE SOCIAL SCIENCES, A GOLD COAST UNIVERSITY

There are only so many hours in the day. This trite observation has not deterred universities from seeking to cram more and more hours in the working week of their already stretched academics. They have done so, as we shall see, by raising workload expectations and adding new elements to the daily grind. The fact that academics are paid for a fixed amount of hours seems irrelevant to universities, which often demand that academics fulfil many of their duties – research, reading, writing – outside the allotted time slots. Arguably, this has always been the case, but something has changed since the late 1980s, and that change is evidenced in a system that requires academics to be more responsive to growing demands of student-shoppers (especially with staff–student ratios having ballooned to an average of 1:34, from about 1:25 in 2000), to manage increasing amounts of administration and red tape, and to respond to the formidable challenges of quality control. Not surprisingly, one of the most persistent and heartfelt complaints among academics interviewed for this book was that of excessive busyness. Most were in fact so busy that they would frequently complain of not having enough time to complain about being busy.

Some academics refer colloquially to such frenetic busyness as 'headless chicken syndrome' or 'HCS', whereby constant regulated motion leads to various psychological problems including anxiety disorders, hypertension and depression. HCS has been known to lead people to drink excessive quantities of cheap red wine, and to turn otherwise tranquil individuals into gibbering wrecks. Some of these symptoms – confirmed in a number of research studies more serious than mine – are behavioural reactions to an organisational culture that places significant, and some say intolerable, demands upon academics, who ultimately buckle under the cumulative pressures. Some cope by complaining to colleagues or resorting to black humour, others take on all the lifeless and resigned features of institutionalised zombies. Others go on sick leave, or leave altogether.

One typical sufferer of HCS, a senior lecturer in social science in Queensland, described his work experience in the following terms:

> There's this sense of perpetual pressure, trying to achieve impossible demands. I often get up in the middle of the night to make lists, often several pages long, of things that need to be done – essays to be marked, students to see, forms to be completed, courses to prepare, articles to write, etc. etc. The thing is, you can never get to what you need to do because other things crop up. Students drop in, or there's a meeting to attend, emails to answer, or some crisis to resolve. It's endless. I don't really have worry-free days, or free weekends.

HCS is rampant throughout Whackademia. Its emergence goes back to the Dawkins reforms and the creation of a mass-market system of higher education. Initially exhibited by an associate professor in Sydney, the disorder has, over the years, been exacerbated through the imposition of intensive work regimes presided over by increasingly powerful administrators and school heads. The saddest subjects of all in this culture of busyness are the 'para-academics': those workers appointed to supposedly academic positions but who end up willingly undertaking excessive amounts of administrative and bureaucratic activities to the exclusion of all else. While they may be rewarded for all their purposeful busyness by gaining promotion (much to the dismay of their more scholarly colleagues), the symptoms of this disorder are so ingrained that they come to resemble public service automatons obsessed with targets, inputs, outputs and impacts. They rarely take tea breaks and are always too busy to engage in friendly conversation. Instead, para-academics can be seen bent over keyboards, rifling through filing cabinets or manically taking notes at meetings. They are old before their time and have flawed relationships with themselves and just about everyone else. Although not yet sectionable under the mental health legislation they are, nonetheless, likely to be noticed by others. Frequently absent on sick leave, they have been known to seek treatment from the occasional sympathetic colleague, campus counsellors, or the university chaplain, although para-academics quickly return to bad habits. Before we reflect on what it's like to live with HCS it might be worth indulging in a little nostalgia. What was it like being an academic in an Australian university say 30 or 40 years ago, before busyness struck? How did academics get along before the emergence of micro-management and workload formulas? Did they have time to lounge around and converse? Was there space to think?

When I was a lad ...

The short answer to the above questions is that universities were very different to today's institutional regimes: at least that's the conclusion drawn by two eminent retired professors who worked in the same Queensland institution for nearly four decades respectively. As we sipped tea and nibbled on crunchy homemade biscuits on the deck of a beautiful Queenslander, I began by asking Professor Smith about what precisely had changed over the years. Were there any conditions resembling HCS in the old days?

A highly intelligent, thoughtful and gentle man, Professor Smith peered into the distance and slowly scratched his balding head. Over the course of a highly successful academic career he had applied his passions for teaching and research, developed new courses and research agendas, headed research centres, and befriended and mentored hundreds, perhaps thousands of students. He was a man immersed in the idea of the activist university as a place of vibrant scholarship and purposeful, non-competitive collegiality: he and his peers simply wanted to make the world a better, more peaceful place. To talk with Professor Smith was to traverse four decades of academic life and political upheaval ranging from the ideological effervescence of the 1960s (anti-war and civil rights movements, non-violent activism and the rest) through the equally active 1970s and early 1980s (protesting against a conservative state government, the threat of nuclear war and the imperialistic ambitions of powerful states), to the rise of neo-liberal conservatism in the mid-1980s and thereafter.

'I think I need to preface my comments', Professor Smith began, with a hint of the mischievous. 'There's a touch of nostalgia in what I am about to say, and I may see the things I want to see in the past. I accept that.' Following a few chuckles he continued:

> I think the first major change I witnessed occurred in the 1970s under the Whitlam government and later, under the Hawke government. It was the growth in numbers of students coming through the system that really brought about the big changes. Suddenly we had to grapple with a lot more students with the same number of staff. We had less time for everything because there were more students to see, more administration, and more essays to mark.

But what did university life look like in the 1960s before the onset of Whitlamite free education and later neo-liberal governance?

> The sixties were really very collegial. We would meet often for coffee in the mornings and afternoons and sit around and talk. We'd talk to people from different departments. There

> was a great spirit of interdisciplinary collegiality and interest. Everyone knew everyone else. When university student numbers grew we lost that sort of interaction. It disappeared very quickly … Before, student numbers were smaller so it was a lot easier to manage, to have time for conversations with one's colleagues. I was also lucky to have a very supportive head of department who basically left me alone to get on with my work. You weren't continually being observed and tested like today. You were trusted. You had pride in doing good work. Sure, a small percentage of tenured academics abused the system but by and large, most worked very effectively without all the scrutiny. We were trusted and respected professionals. It was a good life for us … It was far more productive in terms of doing good research – innovative, ground-breaking research, not like today where there is a lot of repetition because people simply want to publish, to get their work out there rather than do something that might actually bring about change.

Professor Smith spoke too about the importance of tenure in providing a sense of security, and a recognition of work that was judged in relation to one's colleagues rather than imposed by external assessors:

> We all got tenure … If you performed OK you got it. I worked hard because I had pride in what I was doing. Our standing with our colleagues was regarded as the most important thing to measure things by. You didn't want to appear as if you were abusing the system. You wanted respect from your colleagues and the way to gain that was to perform well. We had pride in what we did, and there was always the incentive of promotion of course. But we didn't feel as if we were competing against each other.

For Professor Smith, the most fundamental changes occurred as a result of the introduction of the business model in universities during the mid- to late 1980s:

> The whole atmosphere of universities changed in the 1980s when we had all this business stuff, and an obsession with money-making. There was also a greater sense of being scrutinised by the public. We were increasingly tested on our performance so that a record could be kept of what we were doing. Our sense of freedom vanished. About a quarter of our time was spent filling out forms. We also had to apply for grants so that money could come into the department ... And then there was a major change in terms of how we were expected to mark assignments. Our results had to follow a certain pattern. Eyebrows would be raised if you failed students. You had to conform to the expectation that you pass students. In the sixties academics were not pressured to give students good marks.

The new regulatory regime included the micro-management of academics and was presided over by expanded ranks of administrators. As Professor Smith recalled:

> Not so long ago I saw some figures that outlined the ratio of academics to administrators at the university. The figures spanned about 70 years. As the decades wore on the gap narrowed and in the 1980s and especially 1990s the lines crossed. Now there are more administrators than academics and I understand the situation is getting even worse ... Administrators of course feel compelled to justify their positions and so it was that as the 1980s progressed, academics were obliged to

> fill out more forms – endless amounts of forms. We were required to document what we were doing: how many students we had, how many students we were supervising, and so on. We were no longer trusted. We lost that aura of being professionals. Now the administrators were watching us, scrutinising us ... Even so, I remained content because at least I was teaching and had contact with students. It was still a labour of love ... What changed significantly though was the undermining of collegiality. You felt that you were in direct competition with colleagues. The question was: who could publish the most and teach the best so we could compete for promotion. There was no longer the sense of mutual support we had in earlier times.

As Professor Smith spoke, Professor Jones – a longstanding friend who worked in another department – was like one of those nodding dogs on a car's dashboard. I thought his head might come loose. He agreed with every syllable uttered by his friend: 'Yes, yes', 'That's right', 'Absolutely', 'Indeed'.

I invited Professor Jones to reflect on the introduction of the business model into higher education during the 1980s. He immediately homed in on the vexed matter of quality control – a central pillar in the new order:

> Oh yes, I was on all these committees dealing with teaching and learning. In the end I couldn't stand it. It was ridiculous. What they claimed as quality control – gazing endlessly at student grades and course structures – really had nothing to do with quality. It was all about the appearance of quality. In one of the schools in my faculty, they were obsessed with demonstrating something called quality. They produced a beautiful

> 120-page coloured report which was meant to demonstrate the high quality of their course delivery. The only problem was that the entire department was involved in producing the document and they had no time to do teaching and research!

But what really irked the learned professor was the ceaseless drudgery of quality control, the form-filling, box-ticking and general obsession with monitoring performance. He attributed this to the emergence of an army of freshly empowered administrators:

> The thing that really got to me was the degree to which academics were controlled by administrators and the huge amount of bullshit academics had to confront in the form of so-called quality control. There was loads of this nonsense, and less time for real scholarly work. In my view there is an inverse relationship between the increase in quality control and actual quality education. The former has made the latter a lot harder to achieve because we are constantly staring over our shoulders and filling in stupid forms.

Perhaps the biggest change to have occurred in universities over the past few decades, according to Professor Jones, was the slide in standards. In fact Professors Smith and Jones saw this as an inevitable consequence of the marketisation of higher education, where getting 'bums on seats' became the top priority for frantic university managers. As Professor Jones noted:

> I have taught in universities for over 40 years. The thing I have noticed over this time is that standards have definitely slipped and universities tend to pass people they shouldn't, those who simply aren't up to it. Also the variety of subjects

has gotten smaller and if they don't meet market expectations, they're dropped. We used to teach really small groups because we thought the subject was worth it, not because the market dictates what we should teach.

This tendency to pass people who 'simply aren't up to it' was manifested in the empirical (and highly subjective) obsession with the bell curve. And so it was, said Professor Jones, that the tortured deliberations of various committees on grade distribution (and the exercises in 'moderation' that preceded them) became increasingly anchored in the need to pass rather than fail students – and for good reason, as universities were (and remain) hell-bent on retaining students to offset precarious funding arrangements. Professor Jones again:

> This bloody normal distribution thing is just plain stupid. It took hold in the 1980s. I was always being asked by people at the examiners committee about why a certain number of students had failed or got HDs. What on earth could you say? The score reflected their work, an exceptional cohort? On one occasion when I failed a number of students, my dean rang me up and said he wanted to see me immediately.
>
> He said, 'You can't fail that many people' – it was about 80 per cent.
>
> I asked, 'Why not?'
>
> 'Because you can't', he said.
>
> 'But that reflects the level of work in the group.'
>
> 'I don't care', he replied. He directed me to hand over the assignments and grades to him and he passed the majority of students, even though they had marks as low as 8 per cent! I washed my hands of the whole thing. The same happened

> three years later. Of course, down the track I had colleagues coming up to me and asking me why on earth I passed any of this lot.

Then Professor Jones got back into the 'in my day' routine: 'That just didn't happen in the sixties, that sort of interference. It's much more common now because universities are in a different ball game. They need to keep their students to survive financially. That sort of mind-set changes everything.'

These sorts of observations might be dismissed out of hand by today's university managers as elitist, sentimental drivel, born of resentment of the new corporate reality. Well, if indeed these reflections are drivel then they are shared by all but one of the ten or so older professors I interviewed for this book. Typically, as one globe-trotting senior academic in peace and conflict studies from Victoria observed:

> during the sixties, universities were full of eccentrics and vibrant ideas. There were all sorts of academics hanging around, some published, and others didn't. It didn't seem to matter ... It was what they contributed to debate and argument that mattered. There are very few real characters around these days. Academics are more valued for how much they contribute to revenue streams than to ideas.

As pointed out in later chapters, there is good reason to believe that cut-throat competition, excessive workloads, performance appraisal, and altered pedagogical approaches have had a detrimental impact on today's academics, who generally struggle to meet daily demands of academic work. This onerous grind can have very serious impacts on an academic's well-being and what some blithely call 'job satisfaction'. As we shall see later, the expansion of teaching activities – through on-line courses, increased class sizes and learning support duties, additional marking and administration, a third semester and constant technological innovation – have all taken their toll. An equally worrying aspect of the new reality, however, is the fact that busyness– like defending the university 'brand' discussed in the previous chapter – has had a very real impact on academic freedom.

Busyness, commercialisation and academic freedom

Since the Dawkins reforms of the 1980s, universities have immersed themselves in the world of commercialisation. This is a trend that is likely to accelerate given the current federal government's further deregulation of the higher education sector, which will make it, according to Professor Stephen Parker, vice chancellor at the University of Canberra, 'the world's first large scale de-regulation of undergraduate university places'. The need for universities to survive in the open market has led to a reliance on all manner of funding sourced from research grants, student fees and consulting services. In 2000, in an effort to gauge the impact of such developments on academic freedom, researchers from the Australia Institute interviewed 165 social science academics from a range of city and regional universities. 'Academic freedom' – a slippery term at best – was defined as 'the right to teach, research and publish contentious issues, to choose their own research colleagues and to feel supported by the institution to speak on social issues in areas of their expertise without fear or favour'.

Although there was little direct interference in routine work, academics reported to these researchers that they spent less and less time with their colleagues, and that the competition between them had increased markedly over the years. Of equal concern were a range of systemic effects that impacted on academic freedom. For instance, respondents noted that 'increased workloads, in part arising from writing competitive tenders and developing and marketing commercial courses' had reduced academics' 'independent research time'. These academics also observed that they faced increased pressure to trawl for industry-based funding and external consultancies which, in effect, 'channelled research effort into safe, well-defined areas, rather than speculative or curiosity-driven ones'. In relation to student intake and course delivery, these academics noted that the emergence of full fee-based, vocationally oriented courses for domestic and overseas postgraduate students, and the emergence of market relevant on-line programs more generally, 'sometimes redirected academics' teaching focus to areas tangential to their expertise'. Finally, these respondents maintained that the development of 'corporate management structures' inside universities in order to meet market demand tended to diminish 'collegial decision-making structures'.

Not surprisingly, such commercially generated incursions into academic freedom left the majority of respondents (over 90 per cent) seriously concerned about their work conditions and ability to perform what they regarded as traditional academic duties. Well over two-thirds felt that their academic freedom had been eroded over the years, mainly as a result of the commercialisation of higher education. The report concluded that: 'The consistency of reasons given for systemic concern across the range of disciplines or subject areas and universities (where one would not expect close communication) suggests that some of these issues may be endemic'.

This tends to bear out much of what our retired professors, as well as recent studies by the LH Martin institute, the NTEU and the Centre for the Study of Higher Education, have to say about the changed university environment. It also confirms that the culture of busyness has been presided over by taskmasters whose brief is financial survival through brand protection supported by a disciplined workforce.

Academics, in the meantime, continue to complain about the negative effects of this culture. For instance, in blogged responses to concerns raised about the parlous state of Australian universities in *The Age* last year, the theme of busyness came to the fore. As one blogger, Bry, noted:

> OK, let's look at the options as a fresh young member of academic staff at a well-known university ... You are loaded with responsibilities that have no time constraints: teaching, research, conferences, writing papers, supervising graduate students, committees. Each of these could take up all your time, and it is a superhuman task to try to do them all well. My evenings and weekends were spent working.

In addition to describing Australian universities as 'stuffed' and 'brain dead', Bry suggested that collective action through the National Tertiary Education Union might be the way to begin the process of rolling back some of the worst aspects of university governance. Alex on the other hand, characterised academics as nerdy loners:

> It's hard enough to get them to waste 10 minutes chatting to colleagues in the academic tea-room, never mind organising a defense of universities. People who keep their nose to the grindstone are easily stabbed in the back. Hence the continual increase in workload and class sizes, and resulting decrease in quality – without open protest.

According to another blogger, this also explains 'why so many academics who are unable to organise their way out of a paper bag somehow float up into positions of senior management, while others sink under a load of paperwork'. But the pivotal point for Alex is the expansion of higher education:

> the real difficulty in defending universities these days is that the term itself has lost its meaning. If 40 per cent of the population is to attend university then there is no way that universities can be academically elite institutions. Or perhaps our universities are so dumbed-down that few people who work in them consider them worth saving.

But the question kept popping up: Why don't academics revolt against the system, against hyperactive busyness? Jim had a particular take on this:

> Academics' failure to speak out about the state of universities is hardly surprising when so many (with some marked exceptions) can't even engage with society on their own subject areas. If we need to tell people through advertising that 'universities matter' then perhaps there's a problem ... If academia is seen as a career to be advanced by not rocking the boat, meeting 'performance indicators', by publishing in obscure journals, and getting students to give you high teaching ratings for your lax standards, then why would you stick your neck out to campaign for better universities?

Actually, that's an interesting point. Given the litany of complaints lodged against universities, why would academics want to mount a revolt? Would they even know what they were revolting against, and what would be put in the place of the current system?

While awaiting answers to such questions, academics continue to complain about the culture of busyness in universities and how this has been sustained by a regime of heightened internal scrutiny (at least compared to a few decades ago) and various relational stresses and strains that occasionally arise in the form of industrial action or direct face-offs between academics and faculty administrators. Such tensions arise in part because of the particular hierarchical arrangements that operate in universities. Let's look a little more closely at these structural arrangements.

The university triangle

Universities are formidable hierarchies. At the organisational apex is the university council – responsible for the governance of the university – and senate, which is concerned with academic affairs, although at the University of Queensland the senate's attention is largely restricted to issues concerned with senior appointments, finance, mission and strategic directions, policy and procedural principles, staff performance and general academic matters.

Both senates and councils have broad memberships of appointed and nominated members. They may include businesspeople, local dignitaries, union and student representatives, academics and bureaucrats, heads of key university committees, the vice chancellor, other university managers and senior administrators. Although the composition varies from one institution to another – with some universities seeking to minimise the number of student and academic members – councils and senates together act as a kind of executive committee, setting out or re-affirming the broad institutional goals and what in corporate speak are referred to as 'strategic directions' and 'strategic positioning'.

Of the individual officers, the chancellor is the nominal head of any university, but may or may not have an active involvement in university affairs, choosing instead to leave the day-to-day management to the vice chancellor – the real executive officer – and other senior managers. Sometimes, however, as in the case of the debacle that occurred in 2010 at the University of New England, the chancellor may take on a more active role than that desired by the vice chancellor – in which case all hell breaks loose. Beneath vice chancellors are the pro vice chancellors, who take responsibility for the more specific parts of institutional business like teaching and learning, research, 'global reach', overseas students, 'community engagement' and so forth. Below them are the deans who, along with a number of assistant deans, preside over faculties – sometimes referred to as 'corporate silos'.

Next down the chain are professors and associate professors, then senior lecturers – who tend to float around in a sort of limbo between lecturer and associate professor – while lecturers on various salary scales make up the bulk of full-time academic staff. Lowest of the low in the university's academic hierarchy are the casuals. They are employed under suspect contracts that, in the vast majority of cases, afford them no sick or holiday pay and no right of appeal if they are summarily sacked. Despite some recent advances in pay and conditions, casual staff continue to work under what frequently amounts to ad hoc systems of patronage or what is widely referred to as 'precarious employment'. In effect, this group constitutes a sort of reserve army of what journalist Stephen Matchett describes as 'domestic servants' that undertake the bulk of teaching without any of the perks. As you might expect, some of the most persistent and justifiable complaints in universities emanate from this group.

As noted earlier, school heads – who are accountable to deans and can be appointed from senior lecturer upwards – have various powers bestowed upon them by virtue of their position in the management structure. Their role is to essentially 'line-manage' those under their charge. An array of surveillance practices – probation and performance reviews, 'sign offs' on conference leave, study leave, annual leave and promotion applications and so on – mean that encounters between academic staff and school heads are highly contingent and depend as much on personality and 'style of management' as on official duty statements or policy protocols. Needless to say, a range of outcomes may result in such circumstances, including the differential treatment of staff and a system of patronage, especially when it comes to casuals and sectional staff who often have to rely on little more than the hoped for good will of academics, administrators and the school head. Because of this system, contract workers can often disappear off the scene with alarming rapidity, having upset someone or questioned existing arrangements within a school. By the same token, as we shall see later, keeping one's job in these circumstances may mean having to appear acquiescent and dutiful by conforming to expectations.

Keeping watch

Managerial scrutiny of academics comes in many guises. Obsequious devotees of micro-management – of which there are a significant number among today's university administrations – scrutinise every aspect of each academic's 'performance' and have been encouraged to do so through the rallying cries of 'accountability' and 'transparency'. Most of the watching is top-down, rather than sideways or bottom-up, which means that the rigidity of hierarchical arrangements is regularly reproduced to sustain a given organisational order. The constant watching of time, motion and performance is of course not done equitably – how could it, given the vicissitudes of context and personality? – and has the additional effect of instilling various levels of apprehension among academics.

During the course of an academic's career, he or she may be subject to all manner of watchful rituals: probation periods (up to five years in some cases), performance reviews, student evaluations, oversight from teaching and learning experts, and now the eagle-eyed scrutiny of quality assurance personnel. There are also a dizzying array of general teaching and outcome surveys to endure, as well as routine inquiries by school heads, deans and occasionally pro vice chancellors. Depending on the relationship between scrutiniser and subject, such managerial practices can produce varied and often unpleasant results. Performance reviews seem to strike particular fear into the hearts of academics, perhaps because they play such a major role in determining next year's incremental pay rise and lingering promotion prospects.

Despite all the reassurances from human resources personnel and managerial nods towards 'due process', the fact is that no-one likes the annual performance review, especially those academics who may have already had run-ins with their faculty administrators. In such cases the review is equivalent to ritualised torture. For whatever the performance review claims to be, it is a process deeply enmeshed in top-down power dynamics, that can be applied very differently depending on the relationship struck with one's manager.

For one performance review, I received a report that bore little resemblance to my own appraisal. So incongruent was its assessment of the quality of my work that I thought I had been sent the wrong review. As I glanced through the error-strewn missive, I was astonished by the ability of the author to conjure such a fictional narrative from so poorly informed points of history: innuendo, gossip, circumstantial evidence, gross inaccuracies, simple untruths and other cosmic distortions littered the document. I was confronted by invective masquerading as objective assessment. I stared at the offending document more in amazement than disbelief, but worried about how I might begin to extract myself from this hornet's nest. I was gripped by a sense of impending doom, as if I were about to be hauled off to the Tower and my head impaled on a spike. Suddenly all the university policies – that once appeared so protective of my rights – vanished as I was brought to heel for imagined offences.

I immediately set about writing a frenzied response that ran to 20 passionate pages of moral outrage, denial, and telling my side of the various incidents that I believed had been so skewed in the report. My attempts at self-empowerment were greatly assisted by a union representative who was eventually able to expose this particular review process as nothing more than a vengeful reaction to perceived threats to managerial authority. There were of course several other dimensions to this story – as there always are – but the sense of powerlessness I experienced in a hierarchical system which did not afford me the most basic form of natural justice was, if nothing else, a novel personal experience.

Most universities tinker with their performance review processes, fine-tuning certain elements and introducing new, more creative and expansive ways to monitor academic activity. For instance, as is common in a number of sectors these days, some institutions like Macquarie University have sought to link performance appraisal to financial rewards. The model employs various ranking descriptors – such as 'proficient', 'high achievement', 'excellent', 'partial achievement', and the dreaded 'unsatisfactory'. The ranking of individuals according to this system is highly divisive and, not surprisingly, academic staff at Macquarie resisted its implementation, perhaps objecting to the Pavlovian approach of linking reward to institutional obedience.

Despite such problems, performance reviews in all their manifestations are probably here to stay: the struggle now is to try to ensure some equity and equilibrium is built into the system. Some universities have begun to try out alternative approaches including peer reviews and external mediation. Others have even introduced '360-degree assessment' whereby academic staff can assess the performance of their managers! By and large, however, the current system of review is very much grounded in a hierarchical structure which rests on aspects of organisational life that are simply unavoidable: personal fads and foibles, and subjective preferences and judgments.

This is not to say that the performance review process is without its uses. Applied in a less regulatory and more collegial setting, they can assist academics to negotiate their way through various competing work demands and perhaps to improve some practice elements. But 'performance' is a contested term if ever there was one, not least because it relies on such narrow empirical and highly subjective parameters – at least in the current regulatory system.

One of the most consistent comments I got from academics interviewed for this book was that the performance review process was applied differentially, and occasionally for purposes of base vengeance and pet-like favouritism. As one senior academic from the University of Queensland remarked: 'It all depends where you stand in the school. If you're part of the cabal and follow the orthodoxy then you're OK. If not, you're in trouble.' This differential exercise of power tended to vary over time, with some academics falling in and out of favor with the school head, while others somehow managed to avoid close attention. Additionally, older interviewees argued that younger academics were far more likely to have adopted today's regulatory rationalities, in contrast to more seasoned academics who are perhaps most resistant to the new order. Whether or not this is true is less important than the fact that, to survive and thrive in the current tertiary culture, certain compromises may have to be made – even if this feels at times like putting one's soul out to tender.

Frayed edges

Given the ceaseless surveillance that takes place in most universities, it is hardly surprising that academics exhibit signs of anxiety, fear and stress. Pressure to meet deadlines, administrative demands, research and teaching 'goals' undoubtedly take their collective toll. As noted, academics also complain a lot about over-regulation. In addition to the usual round of reviews, they have to endure glass office walls (as at QUT), heads of school checking on emails (which they are entitled to do), constant checks while 'working at home', diarised records of home-based activities, and insistence that detailed timetables be placed on office doors – failure to do so can result in disciplinary action.

Additionally, there are the various idiosyncrasies of students to contend with. Academics fear students' complaints above all others, as these are typically viewed with great concern by school heads. After all, the customer is always right. At the very least the academic in question may have to answer a 'please explain' in writing to the school head, and then perhaps be grilled directly on one or more occasion until an 'appropriate' action is decided upon. An unsatisfactory outcome can result in a sinister paragraph or two in one's performance review report and/or a referral to a teaching and learning expert for urgent remedial action.

Either way, academics find themselves wedged between the rock of consumer satisfaction and the hard place of managerial governance. And there's no escaping the rock. On-line or 'distance' education means that academics can now be accessed day or night by increasingly needy students, some with inquiries that border on the banal ('Do you mind if I use sub-titles?', 'Do you want me to staple my assignment?', 'Can I use Times New Roman?', 'My baby spilt custard all over the assignment cover. It looks like puke but can I still post it to you?'). On top of all this there are on-line forms for just about everything, and these have to be completed according to rigidly set deadlines that suit administrators rather than academics. So how do academics fare in this sort of pressure-cooker situation? Not very well, by all accounts.

Over a decade ago, in a national survey of stress levels among over 3500 continuing academic staff and 4714 other staff in 17 Australian universities, Professor John Winefield and his colleagues concluded that over half of the former group were 'at risk of psychological illness, compared with only 19 per cent of the Australian population overall'. Job satisfaction – taken as a key indicator of stress – was low among academics compared to other occupational groups (nurses, school teachers, engineers etc). The majority of academics stated they were unhappy with university management, hours of work, industrial relations, chances of promotion, and rates of pay. Lecturers and senior lecturers involved in teaching and research activities, especially those working in humanities and social sciences at the newer universities, suffered the most psychological strain as a result of low job satisfaction. Nearly a third of academics worked over 55 hours a week. The factors that predicted high levels of stress were job insecurity and work demands. The happiest campers had more autonomy, less gripes with their bosses and a sense of procedural fairness. Generally though, academics did not hold much faith in senior management or the promise of procedural fairness. Winefield and his colleagues concluded that:

> Australian university staff, particularly academic staff, highly stressed. Diminishing resources, increased teaching loads and

> student/staff ratios, pressure to attract external funds, job insecurity, poor management and a lack of recognition and reward are some of the key factors driving the high level of stress.

You might think that this study is old hat: after all, it was undertaken in the year 2000. Surely things have improved? In a follow-up study of 13 universities conducted in 2003 and 2004, Winefield and his colleagues found some positive results overall, with academic staff reporting more commitment to their universities, more job involvement, autonomy and procedural fairness, more trust in senior management, and less work pressure and job insecurity. All good news?

Not quite. The positive changes for academics were small when compared with the gloomy findings of the earlier survey, and were certainly less positive than the administrative staff – for whom things seemed to have improved across most areas. Quite why this should be the case was not entirely clear, although the authors noted that 'procedural' and other changes initiated by university managements had built trust and a greater sense of security among all workers, although more so for administrative staff. There was also evidence among academic staff of an increase in psychological strain and conflict between work and home life, prompting the authors to comment that 'the high and increasing levels of psychological strain, as well as the increased levels of work-home conflict, suggest that the introduction of more flexible work practices for both men and women might need to be addressed next'.

What this seemed to suggest – and we have to be cautious here since Winefield's second study was a lot smaller and less concise that the first – is that academics continue to experience serious challenges in both their workplace and home life, and that they are likely to continue to do so into the future. Given the likelihood of a rapidly rising student intake from 2012, the trend toward even more quality assurance procedures, and greater market competition from the over 150 private providers of higher education, acute stress levels will undoubtedly intensify in the coming years. And remember, Winefield's study did not to include the most exploited and vulnerable group of academics of all – casuals.

This omission was addressed in a more recent study of over 5000 academics across 20 universities conducted by the Centre for the Study of Higher Education at the University of Melbourne, published in 2011. This study came to conclusions strikingly similar to previous reports, affirming the occurrence of continued high levels of stress brought about by unmanageable workloads, 'disquiet with leadership and management', and concerns over job security and income levels. About half of those interviewed indicated their intention to retire, gain employment in overseas universities or move to another profession. As the report concluded:

> Many academics indicate that they are struggling to manage existing workloads. While the findings suggest that the satisfaction academics gain from their scholarly activities to some extent mitigates problems related to working conditions, protecting the future quality of teaching and research will require careful consideration of work design, workloads and working conditions.

An exclusive report on this study in *The Australian* – headed 'Harried underpaid staff plan to flee the sector' – noted particular dissatisfaction over pay and conditions among casual staff as well as more generalised concerns over the level of monitoring of staff. One of the authors of the report, Dr Emmaline Bexley noted that 'we got a lot of feedback on how much time staff spend simply accounting for how they spend their time'. This, along with various other pressures, the report noted, had resulted in significant levels of job stress and dissatisfaction. Significantly, the study noted that the removal of caps on student places and a more rigorous approach to quality assurance was likely to deepen many of the negative feelings of both continuing and casual academics.

Gauging quality

Mention quality assurance to most academics and they will wince – and for good reason. Quality assurance is the latest and most formidable regulatory incursion into job performance in the post-Dawkins era. Like the grand inquisitions carried out in other educational sectors, quality assurance has the capacity to strike terror into the hearts of even the most hardened academics.

The latest government pitch for quality comes from the *Review of Australian Higher Education: Final Report* published in 2008, otherwise known as the Bradley report. A turgid document dedicated to promoting the values of mass-market higher education, it somehow manages to by-pass any meaningful reference to academics as human beings (other than making a few bland comments about workload 'pressures', lousy pay and aging employees, all under a section titled 'Working conditions reduce attractiveness'). The real concern of the Bradley report is to develop a system of higher education that complements the market-based ethos of flexible course delivery and consumer choice, and which would require even more measurement of 'performance outcomes' and 'impacts'. Or, in the stifling diction so beloved of the managerial class: 'The more demand-driven, student-entitlement system will require a greater focus on accreditation, quality assurance, evaluation of standards and use of outcomes measures'.

Already nervous about how much they are scrutinised, academics might be justified in feeling apprehensive about such plans. But the Bradley report insists that:

> Placing more choice in the hands of students requires a different approach to quality assurance and accreditation. A national system for accreditation of all higher education providers – both public and private – on a regular cycle is necessary to assure the quality of the deregulated system.

Quality in this deregulated system will, according to the Bradley report, involve regular and repeated bouts of detailed examination, the likes of which have yet to be experienced in the university sector. This will entail 'more rigorous application of revised and strengthened National Protocols for Higher Education Approval Processes, coupled with a quality assurance framework based on externally validated standards and rigorous measures of performance'. In other words, deregulation for the student-shopper will require increased regulation of the academics on the shopfloor.

This regulatory approach is to be underpinned by what amounts to a carrot-and-stick approach to funding:

> As part of this new approach to quality assurance, targets relating to quality of teaching will be agreed with each higher education provider in receipt of Commonwealth Government funds. Some 2.5 per cent of the grants for teaching and learning annually will be quarantined for payment on achievement of these targets.

In effect, a system of rewards and punishments orientated around the goal of quality assurance will provide the framework for university governance in the twenty-first century. Previous (presumably unaccountable) approaches to higher education will accordingly become a thing of the past.

And what better way to bring academics to heel than by introducing a new national assurance body to oversee the new order: TEQSA, which stands for the Tertiary Education Quality and Standards Agency. Charged with responsibility for registering and de-registering universities, accrediting and or de-accrediting courses, evaluating the performance of universities and programs, the monitoring and enforcement of compliance procedures, and encouraging best practice, TESQA is set to expose the innards of every university across Australia. Academics will, as never before, find themselves exposed to the scrutiny of external assessors with unprecedented powers of monitoring and review. Yet in the search for 'capacity building', 'inclusiveness' and 'transparency' – all by-words for quality – the architects of TESQA appear to have completely disregarded the impact of this new regulatory regime will have on academics who already labour under the dead-weight of institutional scrutiny.

If there are any lingering doubts that TESQA has highly penetrative powers, consider Jonathon Ross's interview with Professor Bradley in a 2011 issue of *Campus Review*, in which she said that the agency would focus on the bottom 20 per cent of universities, and that the agency would have powers to 'intervene at the course, student cohort, institution and sector levels and to scrutinise whole institutions as well as particular aspects of their operations'.

Such intentions are bound to have profound impacts on an already disaffected academic workforce. Significantly over-regulated, stressed-out and disillusioned already, it seems academics are about to face yet another layer of managerial scrutiny – all in the name of student choice, excellence, quality, best practice – or whatever. Academics will find themselves in the full glare of public scrutiny, like reluctant pole-dancers cavorting to rhythms not of their making. Experience of similar inquisitions elsewhere tells us that once a TEQSA-like body has swung into action, morale among academics will further decline and many will flee the profession. This exodus has in fact already started, but TEQSA's inquisitorial existence may well hasten the process.

You might wonder why the Bradley higher education review did not more fully consult with those likely to be most affected by the proposed changes – namely academics. In fact, in proposing a huge expansion of the student intake, the Bradley review ignored the capacity of academics to deliver the high-quality education envisaged. Quite simply, there are likely to be too few of them to do so unless there is a massive infusion of government funding. As Honorary Professorial Fellow of the LH Martin Institute, Vin Massaro, commented in *The Australian* not long after the Bradley report was released in 2009, it made no mention of the possibility of recruiting the academic workforce necessary to teach the enlarged student cohort. Massaro estimated that with the staff–student ratio of 1:20, an additional 18 000 staff would be required 'at a time when the academic workforce is shrinking'.

Given the fact that academics are likely to experience increased pressures as a result of the Bradley report's proposals, it might be worth remembering the damage done to the morale of British teachers when bodies similar to TESQA were introduced in that country in the 1990s. The profession was left reeling, and thousands of teachers felt overwhelmed and often terrified by what appeared like overzealous scrutiny of their performance.

Whether or not such regulatory exercises improve the quality of teaching and learning remains very much open to question. The fact remains that academics and universities in general are now scrutinised more than ever before, and universities seem to fall over themselves in an effort to introduce new and more sophisticated surveillance technologies aimed at teaching and other areas of work. In 2011 the Department of Education, Employment and Workplace Relations proposed three new forms of teaching evaluation, while individual universities are constantly developing their own in-house schemes. One wonders if the proponents of such initiatives ever realise what impact this increased surveillance has on the capacity of academics to actually carry out their core duties – and to remain sane. It seems not. In the next chapter, I consider the growing pressures of teaching on academics, and the questionable practices adopted by universities to manufacture 'excellence' in this regard.

4

Production-line teaching

I love teaching students – well most of them. But the stress of having to do everything else means there's no time to really think about teaching … I also found that by letting people in who couldn't really write essays or think critically, I found it hard to deal adequately with the spread of student talent or to teach the critical stuff I wanted to … Sometimes it was a case of how low did I need to pitch my teaching so that most students could begin to learn.

LECTURER IN CRIMINOLOGY, WESTERN AUSTRALIA

Students are taught but they don't learn. The teaching is all very mechanical and linked to particular aims and objectives. You put up the slides, put your lecture notes on-line, make sure you cover everything in the unit guide so that your arse is covered.

SENIOR ACADEMIC IN LEGAL STUDIES, QUT

Enthusiastic promoters of the contemporary university would have us believe that the practice of teaching in these institutions is a finely tuned and highly professional activity that produces life-altering 'learning outcomes' which can be recorded and conveniently slotted into a student's embossed portfolio. The reality, of course, is a little different. Like most activities in universities, teaching is carried out in the context of extraordinary busyness brought about by overarching demands – especially the burden of having to deal with increasingly large numbers of students. This growth in numbers has been occasioned over the years by various factors: the amalgamation of various educational institutions, the rapid rise of overseas students, and malleable enrollment policies – including lowering entry scores and extremely generous credits.

Such developments have increased the teaching workloads of academics already struggling to keep on top of their other duties. Faced with large numbers of often semi-literate students – many of whom also require intensive remedial education, guidance on how to read books, formulate arguments, reference their work and participate in tutorials – academics now spend more time than ever in 'student contact'.

Particular challenges arise in respect of students with low entry scores and overseas students. As a number of studies have indicated, such is the reliance of universities on the latter group for income-generating purposes that many of them are being allowed to pass units despite the fact that their English is poor. Moreover, notwithstanding the best efforts of learning assistance specialists (and the fact that staffing levels of language support personnel has not kept pace with the increase in overseas students), it appears that many of the overseas graduates who take up employment in this country continue to struggle with English language skills. For instance, in a 2009 survey conducted by Australian Education International (the international wing of the Department of Education, Employment and Workplace Relations), 101 Australian employers were canvassed about the quality of the overseas graduates whom they had employed. Alarmingly, it was noted that 21 per cent thought that English competence among graduates born overseas was 'poor' and that this had a significant impact on written and oral communication and other work-related skills. Clearly, despite extensive remedial work, it is still possible to graduate from an Australian university without the communication skills required to perform some of the most basic employment duties.

Fortunately, the wonders of computer spelling and grammar checks have enabled many students to present their work in a readable form, although serious concerns remain over the ability of large numbers of students to think, write and express themselves in a clear and coherent fashion. This situation has not been assisted in recent times by the emergence of what I have termed 'corset assessment' – whereby pages of instructive notes accompany assessment items guiding students along every step of the way. In one case, a senior psychology academic in a New South Wales university provided 13 pages of guide notes for a 1500-word report!

Equally de-intellectualising has been the development of assessment items like multiple-choice exams and quizzes which, in effect, serve only to assess short-term memory recall and work against the construction of detailed and coherent argument. In some institutions these truncated assessments have begun to replace essays which, in contrast, require students to explore their thoughts and ideas in some depth. But faced with inarticulate essays that can take hours to mark, academics are understandably tempted to seek out assessment methods that require minimum input, usually in the form of ticks and numerical scores.

The communication problems of students make for very difficult teaching, even in an institutional context that prides itself on 'inclusivity', 'flexible delivery' and 'pedagogical excellence'. But the emergence of bigger classes, distance education, unit standardisation, third semesters and new computer technologies have turned teaching into a grueling affair. To be sure, some excellent teaching goes on in universities, and I'm sure many – perhaps most – of those receiving teaching awards deserve them. But as one Sydney academic put it, 'this occurs in spite and not because of the organisational cultures within which academics work'.

Busyness and teaching

The 'busyness' noted in the previous chapter is especially prevalent in the area of teaching. This is because academics are trying – and often failing miserably – to balance this core activity with a host of other demands like administration, research and professional service. More than anything else, it is the extra administration that really gets to academics. As an RMIT law lecturer put it:

> When it comes to teaching there are a host of logistical difficulties. We have great students and it's a joy teaching them. But I can never devote as much time as I'd like to preparation of lectures and tutorials. Everything is done on the run ... It's the paperwork and accountability mechanisms that really impact on us. We're already busy enough and yet we have to contend with various administrative demands which make teaching very difficult.

So disillusioned was this academic that she was seriously thinking of chucking in the towel on teaching:

> I'm thinking of moving out of teaching because I can't cope with the over 80 per cent of time I spend on administration. In fact we spend a lot of time just trying to make sure that students are enrolled properly. But accountability is a big chunk of what we do. Administrators have no real idea about what we do or the challenges of teaching, but we have to understand what they do because there is so much administration foisted upon us ... I am always chasing people in administration trying to do this or that, obtaining the right forms or getting the right information.

Busyness, it seemed, was choking the very life out of this academic:

> Every time I meet a colleague they say 'Oh, I'm so busy'. Everyone says it. It [busyness] crowds out everything we would like to do as academics. We are now teaching in blocks to suit flexible delivery. The course I am currently teaching used to run for a whole semester, now it's taught in six weeks. With all the administration there is no time for reflection, thinking. We're always confronted by deadlines that have to be met. And there are no longer any breaks. I start preparing courses right after the teaching ends. It's impossible.

The same sentiment came up time and again among my respondents. An academic at Macquarie University – on the verge of emotional collapse – remarked:

> It's gone admin crazy!! I just can't keep up with all the rubbish ... I love aspects of my job like teaching but I have great difficulty in keeping on top of all the administrative demands. It has definitely got a lot worse over the past four years, at least

> since I started. The paperwork is incredible. It's all about data collection to satisfy the demands of incentive-based performance funding requirements. They want evidence of everything. On the one hand there is a demand for us to teach and publish, but also to demonstrate that we have indeed published what we say we have, and so we have to copy the articles, fill in detailed forms, and send them to administration … Academic work gets pushed into the background. There's so little time to think and prepare for teaching.

Another disaffected lecturer, this time from the University of Queensland, told me:

> It's the technology that allows this busy culture to happen. There's software for everything these days. It's academics who now have to do the administration because it's on-line and it's expected of us. There's always something you've missed. We used to get admin support to do this. Now the admin people say 'Well, it's on the system'. Oh yeah, thanks for all your help. There's just no room to think. You're continually trying to keep up with all this administrative nonsense. There's simply no time to do the core business like teaching and research.

But it isn't only full-time academic staff who feel overwhelmed by administrative demands. Casual academics – who undertake half or more of tertiary teaching – also find themselves under the lash of busyness. Often undertaking post-graduate studies, casual staff find themselves immersed in the multifarious demands of teaching-related responsibilities. As one contract worker from a university in South Australia observed:

> You get swept into a whole array of menial tasks that aren't properly catalogued in the workload document. Things like keeping records, entering grades on the computer, re-marks, endless student inquiries, announcements on notice boards, responses to flare-ups on discussion boards, completion of forms for the board of assessors, identification of at-risk students and what you are doing to assist them – all these things and more take time, and certainly detract from one's teaching. Things like pay sheets have to be entered on the bloody computer. You have to keep records of how many hours you have worked and then slot this information into little boxes. It all takes time. It's worse of course if you are a unit assessor, as many casual staff are, because you have to keep records of this and that ... All this is done in addition to things like student consultations and the things that arise on a day-to-day basis. There's precious little time to think and read and reflect.

Like their permanent colleagues, casuals are drawn into an organisational culture in which busyness is almost an end in itself, and where intellectual activities are often considered marginal to the daily grind. As an experienced social science casual from a regional university in Victoria commented:

> What's it like being a casual? I can't put it into words. 'Outrageous' comes to mind. Firstly I made more money years ago when I was doing menial jobs than I do now as a casual at a regional university. Secondly, the university is actively anti-intellectual. One of the main things I will remember about my experience is that I had to read books behind closed doors because reading books was seen by administrators and management alike as being inefficient. Being busy is what

> counted. What counted as work was box ticking and trying not to fuck up. I was told by academics and administrators to do the minimum needed.

For this casual employee, the work culture in his university appeared antithetical to intellectual practice, particularly when it came to teaching. What he, along with other casuals, found especially troubling was the arbitrary nature of school governance:

> There was arbitrary allocation of units, many of which I had never taught before. Once you managed to gather a bit of expertise in a unit, you were moved to another one, without any real explanation or recognition that this might cause problems or indeed be inefficient. When I first came to work as a casual I have to admit I was idealistic. I loved teaching and really wanted to make use of the knowledge and skills I possessed. I worked hard and did what I had to do. But I was faced by this arbitrary culture, arbitrary governance. I felt totally powerless.

Teaching 24-7

For the vast majority of academics I spoke to, one of the most daunting aspects of their teaching responsibilities related to distance education, and especially the demands generated by on-line communication. According to a senior QUT academic, this has led to a culture of 'never-ending teaching' where, as soon as one course is completed, 'the administrative demands of another are immediately upon you'. She sheeted this home to internet technology:

> There's been a blow-out in teaching responsibilities brought on mainly by the on-line technology. In fact there's no end to

> teaching-related duties these days. You have to also conform to what the bureaucrats want. In January you have to prepare all your sites and make sure they are uploaded by a certain date. This is all before semester starts ... And then once everything is loaded you have to keep on top of discussion boards, update and change information, and answer endless email inquiries from students.

As we spoke I could see my interviewee gradually sink into a familiar, slumped posture. Her eyes seemed deeper set, the facial lines more pronounced. Luckily we were in a wine bar, so I quickly ordered more white wine. 'Go on', I prompted.

> Oh yes ... then you have to do the actual teaching ... But that's only a small fraction of what we do. The work has gotten worse over the years. It's all the on-line stuff. Most of the time I am very frazzled just trying to keep up with all the demands. I can never get things done, there's always something else to do on top of what you are already doing. Most of my work is teaching-related, preparing units, putting stuff like study guides on line, checking and responding to student's comments on discussion boards – and those are endless. And they start at the beginning of the year, well before semester starts. I spend much more time at the computer than I did say ten years ago. I used to just turn up and talk to the students. But now the technology and bureaucratic system supporting it requires – no, demands – conformity. All our websites have to be the same. It's all very mechanistic, although no-one has discussed whether this is a good thing or not.

This could have been any of my respondents talking.

One young academic in sociology in Sydney kept apologising for 'complaining'. 'I really shouldn't, it's not that bad.'

'But', I pointed out, 'you seem to be working very hard. You said earlier that you arrived at your office at six this morning and that yesterday you worked into the early hours.'

'Yes, I do that a lot ... I can't keep up with it all. I'm new to this and maybe it will get better once I have prepared all my units. But I do find it hard to keep on top of all the teaching demands.'

'Like what?', I inquired.

'You know, the student inquiries, the preparation, all on top of everything else.'

The introduction of a third semester – lauded by university managers as yet another example of 'flexible delivery' – is in fact just another strategy to generate money. One professor in Brisbane remarked tersely that: 'I fucking hate all this teaching. As soon as one semester is completed another one is on top of us. I have barely any time to do research these days, not at all in fact.'

This seemed a bit odd, so I asked 'How come they don't make more use of your reputation and skills as a long-standing and respected academic? It seems counter-intuitive.'

'Well', said the professor, raising his hands in the air, 'you tell me.'

To be sure, many universities employ (guess who?) casuals to do most of the teaching during the period – roughly from early December to mid-February – that was once reserved for research and writing. But full-time academics still have to prepare material, appoint suitable staff and oversee the entire process. They are often drawn into issues that arise during this time, and are contactable via email or mobile phone. Vacating one's office or throwing the mobile phone into a bin are some of the means of temporarily avoiding such pressures, but ultimately, there's no escape from teaching-related commitments – students are very adept at hunting you down.

Stock standard

As exhausting as teaching responsibilities can be, most academics I spoke to expressed the greatest angst over the emergence of standardisation – the practice of seeking consistency in the form and content of teaching-related practices. Standardisation has been vigorously applied by bureaucrats to all aspects of teaching activity. There are many examples, but the one that immediately comes to mind, and which above all reflects the bureaucratic impulse to standardise everything, is the unit information guide.

On the surface, unit information guides may seem benign enough. Their covers are invariably emblazoned with university crests, logos, computer-generated images and various other adornments. But the decoration is just that, and the institutional branding the real give-away: these guides are treated by universities with biblical reverence and as portals to the splendours of standardised education. All aspects of unit content are to be delivered within the parameters of the guide, otherwise students may complain or even take legal action – or at least that's what academics are led to believe. In most universities there is a standard template for such documents, and any changes to the script, which can run to dozens of pages, have to be approved by higher authority – hence the tendency of many academics to make only the most rudimentary alterations.

Academic staff can spend inordinate lengths of time agonising over the contents of unit guides. In addition to cross-tabulated 'unit aims', 'learning objectives' and 'graduate attributes', and the usual declarations of pedagogical excellence, these documents typically include information on plagiarism and extension policies, study plans, contact details, learning support, website addresses and reading lists – each of which contributes to the centrally planned homogenisation of education, and to the workloads of the hapless academics meant to deliver it.

Character assessments masquerading as 'graduate attributes' are a relatively recent addition to unit information guides. They include serious-sounding qualities – like 'critical reflection', 'intellectual rigour', 'ethical understanding' and 'effective communication' – that the student will hopefully attain as a result of taking a particular unit. They are also intended as general intellectual and ethical assessments, and in particular as evidence of job-readiness for prospective employers.

The actual process by which particular constellations of attributes are decided upon by academics is a story in itself. It is largely a mix-and-match affair, in which academics scrutinise each others' selections to make sure there is no repetition across units. In some schools this sifting exercise takes place in staff meetings, so as to avoid protracted negotiations between individual academics. At other times, attributes are selected on their own merits and then placed with great solemnity into the awaiting template that includes unit aims and objectives. Some brave souls have sought to question the inclusion of such attributes on the grounds that they raise ethical concerns, are patronising and/or tend to reflect the vocational orientation of today's universities. Generally though, academics acquiesce to the prevailing orthodoxy. No-one wants to be a troublemaker.

The main – but false – assumption associated with unit guides in general is that students actually take the time to decipher their contents. My own experience is that the majority of students head straight for the assessment items – usually in an effort to calculate the minimum effort required – then briefly backtrack to the aims, and perhaps objectives, but they invariably give graduate attributes a major swerve. I once took the opportunity of asking some of my social work students if they had read their unit guide, and the answer was a resounding no. That said, one or two of the more studious types would at some point burrow into these convoluted documents, mainly in the hope that this might put them one step ahead of their peers. The majority, however, take unit guides for what they are – examples of institutional pedantry and information overload. Clearly, there is an inverse relationship between the effort put into producing unit guides and the time allocated by students to reading them, but this is the last thing the pedants in teaching and learning would want academics to know.

Not surprisingly, the joys of creative, passionate and relevant pedagogy are severely constricted by such institutional straitjackets. Mary, a senior lecturer in social sciences, remarked:

> The bottom line is that, if you have to adhere to the unit outline, your teaching is reduced to simply imparting information. It's not teaching as such. There's an art to teaching and it doesn't come through the strictures of the outline or learning objectives.

Perhaps today's academics should instead take a leaf out of the book of a former QUT lecturer who objected to the stodgy, standardised nature of the guides dictated by his institution, and instead chose to use different typefaces, sizes and colours of font, pictures, cartoons, poems and jokes to liven up his document – which his admiring students read avidly. It's worth noting that this academic ran a very tight ship in terms of his approach to teaching, but refused to be dragged into the quagmire of conformity so heavily advocated by teaching and learning personnel. Understandably, this rebel – who has now retired – became something of a legend in some academic circles.

Rigidification

Equally concerning to the academics I spoke to was what one senior academic at Griffith University referred to as the 'rigidification of pedagogy' – an unappealing spin-off of standardisation. This involves the attempt by teaching and learning experts and academics themselves to ensure a largely pre-determined approach to learning – one that is linked directly to 'learning objectives' set out in unit information guides. These can act as a kind of pedagogical straitjacket requiring academics to adhere to what is stated in the guide. Frequently, as noted below, academics are politely reminded by vigilant students of the fact that they may have skipped over or entirely ignored one or more of the learning objectives. In more serious cases, students may lodge complaints with school heads or write directly to the dean or vice chancellor. Not surprisingly, many of those I talked to expressed particular concern about the tyranny of learning objectives which have led to what a senior lecturer in psychology – let's call him Harry – referred to rather dramatically as the 'death of teaching'.

A softly spoken academic from the mid-west of the United States, Harry has worked in a number of Australian universities and was passionately committed to Socratic pedagogy – that is, a dialogistic encounter between academic and student that involves the vigorous pursuit of knowledge and understanding. He was certainly not someone prone to exaggeration or hyperbole. As we sat in a Gold Coast cafe, I witnessed a mildly contorted look of both sadness and anger cross his face as he spoke of the transformation of higher education from 'intellectual engagement' to a process resembling an 'assembly line'. His take on high-achieving students is interesting:

> I honestly think that the best students get the most out of university education through their own efforts and not what

> is taught to them. If you can inspire a student he or she will go off and do what is needed to learn what they need to know. My role is to help them to think about thinking, so that they can reflect on the world around them. But these days students are constricted by what's in the unit outlines, as are the lecturers. They are given a textbook, lectures on-line – usually mandated by university requirements – restricted amounts of weekly reading, maybe two chapters. The problem for the lecturer is that his or her teaching in the classroom is constricted by learning outcomes – that is, the knowledge that teaching and learning people and others think the student should have at the end of the course. As long as the names, dates and principles are taught to students, then the learning outcomes have been met. That's basically the knowledge that governs this process.

In short, added Harry, 'learning objectives are rigid and formulaic'. But he hadn't finished:

> As far as assessment is concerned, well, my assessment items had to go through a gauntlet of examiners who knew next to nothing about my course, and then the head of school would get involved. All my essay questions had to be in line with the learning objectives. The lack of room and movement for academics really saddens me. There is little respect for us as professionals. Having to confront this sort of bureaucratic culture is so dispiriting. I feel totally disillusioned. My spirit has gone.

This sense of malaise occasioned by the rigidification of university teaching was common to the vast majority of my respondents. A senior academic from one of Australia's private universities observed that:

> Teaching has now become largely an administrative affair with spontaneity going out of the window. The content of lectures is now scrutinised by teaching and learning experts who were probably lousy teachers themselves. Teaching and learning committees have become the new Gestapo. They scrutinise everything and they go out of their way to put everything into a template. This results in the rigidification of education for both academics and students. Sure, teaching can be improved, but you don't need this endless form of scrutiny. No-one has yet demonstrated to me that certain forms of assessment are necessarily better than others, or that there is a right way to do things. For instance, I'm not sure that the written form is always the best way to go and those other genres like film or whatever might be better.

Yet another academic, this time from one of Melbourne's larger universities, noted how lecturers were constrained by the rigidity of learning objectives and the fact that students had become avid consumers, demanding value for money and adherence to what is promised in unit guides as if they were product catalogues:

> Teaching and learning specialists claim they are measuring our teaching. They take a highly quantitative approach but this doesn't reflect what it is we are doing in the classroom, not at all. Everything is linked to 'learning outcomes' and 'competencies', and we are assessed against these sorts of things. It's really about ensuring conformity to the prevailing order. As a lecturer you feel incredibly boxed in. There's no opportunity to be creative. All that has been stamped out of us. If you want

> to introduce new ideas or bodies of knowledge you can't, because you're meant to stick to what has been set in the guide.

This academic was an advocate of 'embodied learning', in which 'you share ideas, information about yourself and what you have learnt and the context in which this learning occurs'. The problem with the current system, he reflected, 'is that students constantly want their units to be delivered according to what is stated in the given outline, they regard higher education as a product'.

For many academics, however, irritation over 'contract education' was hugely outweighed by their opposition to the interventions of teaching and learning experts. An academic in political science was forthright about such matters:

> It's bloody ridiculous how much input [other] people have into our units. Most of them, especially the teaching and learning specialists, have no idea what they're talking about, since they haven't got a clue about the content of what we teach and how this might relate to how we assess students. They obsess about assessment, but there's more to teaching and learning than that.

'Like what?', I inquired.

'Building good, constructive dialogical relations with students, getting them to appreciate what learning means in practice, getting them out of their formulaic headspace.'

Ironically, however, the most startling confession came from a South Australian lecturer in a teaching and learning centre – usually seen by academics as the root of the rigidification evil. I was shocked. I had fully expected her to rally to the defense of all things bureaucratic, but no.

> We're meant to be designing inclusive curricula, but it is also demanded that we do a one-size-fits-all approach. The problem is that people who oversee teaching and learning tend to ignore the fact of living information and that there is no single best way of doing things. They tend to insist that there is only one way of doing things and it leads to what I would call a vanilla sort of approach. It all becomes very rigid and formulaic. Instead of trying to do things the same way we should be looking at the best methods of teaching and learning for that particular group, and every group is different. There's all this talk of inclusivity but it works against teaching in a spontaneous, innovative way. It lacks spark. If you teach to a script then it becomes drudgery, teaching then gets reduced to the imparting of information rather than critical learning.

The feeling that flexibility, creativity and imagination had been stifled by bureaucratic rigidification means that some academics have adopted what they consider to be subversive practices, including 'weaning' or 'resocialising' students away from the constraints of narrowly conceived education. One senior psychology academic from a Brisbane university commented that 'rather than just following an information guide, I would engage with students on things of current interest and try to get them to engage in argument and debate; to think and to articulate their thoughts'. Most students, he insisted, 'haven't been exposed to philosophical arguments and ideas or logic, so they really have no clear idea of what it means to engage in critical reflective thinking'. I was intrigued. Did the attempt at resocialisation work?

> Yes, the students enjoyed what I was doing and I still get letters today from students thanking me for the approach I

> took to teaching ... I tried to get students to think about the relevance of what they were learning in terms of everyday life. I wanted them to become questioning members of society and to think critically about the world they live in.

A laudable aim, surely?

The ceaseless gaze

Perhaps more than any other area of academic life, teaching 'performance' has come in for the inquisitorial scrutiny. There's no Grand Inquisitor as such – although, as mentioned in the previous chapter, the new federal body TEQSA could well become the next Torquemada. For the moment, the scrutiny of individual academics in matters pedagogical comes from a motley but sizeable collection of school heads, teaching and learning experts, external assessors and peers. The focus of this collective gaze varies from one school to another, but more often than not it involves assessing the 'fit' between unit aims, objectives, graduate attributes and assessment items. Less often is the process concerned with the actual content of the unit or its underlying epistemological assumptions. Students are also encouraged to gaze and comment upon units throughout and at the end of each semester and boards of assessors may question the failure to fully 'integrate' assessment items or worse, 'abnormal' grade distributions

Student evaluations and surveys are among the most important elements in any university's system of teaching and learning review. That's why almost every institution goes to extraordinary lengths to ensure that the process is raked over for internal consistency and 'reliability'. Both staff and students are given copious quantities of information and advice on how to approach and reflect upon the educational process. For instance, the University of Tasmania's 'Student Evaluation of Teaching and Learning' webpage contains a truckload of information about teaching evaluation for both staff and students. The staff site includes all manner of information relating to how academics might go about evaluating the reception of their teaching by students. The student site, on the other hand, contains a mass of information dealing with 'feedback from staff on changes made to unit assessment, content and delivery as a direct result of previous evaluations'. The implication seems to be that, if you don't like a course, complain about it and the university will fix it. The customer is always right, after all.

Unit and course evaluations are only part of the great panoply of evaluations that cut across all undergraduate and postgraduate courses. The results of unit evaluations, say the UTAS teaching and learning experts, are public and 'used in Quality Assurance processes throughout the University'. We are told that a head of school or course co-ordinator can request an evaluation at any time, as can the individual unit co-ordinator. Further, unit evaluations can take place more than once during the semester. Such 'flexibility' apparently exists to enable staff members to reflect on their teaching methods and to assess the efficacy of new material. That's the official line of course. But academic staff know better about the many uses to which evaluations are put: sometimes for enlightenment, often for regulatory and punitive purposes. Certainly, when performance reviews are conducted, teaching comes in for very close scrutiny.

For the academic, much depends on positive feedback to their teaching, especially from students. An academic's promotion prospects, and even continued employment, can be jeopardised by a series of negative student evaluations, even from the small minority of students who complete these usually on-line forms. Universities take student evaluations very seriously indeed. The question is why? After all, they are rarely if ever subject to a process of ethical review or to detailed critical scrutiny, other than to fix some technical hitches and/or to alter questions. As objective measurement tools, student evaluations and student experience surveys are about as useful as bed sores. An astute law professor from Sydney, let's call him Eric, damns the credibility of such surveys:

> Student evaluations are useless. You get these small samples and the responses are taken as gospel by management. You couldn't publish this stuff in a respected journal. The samples are way too small and the results are grossly biased. These sorts of surveys simply have no credibility, but in the university context they are taken as gospel. I have been marked down by students because they said the unit was too hard. The thing is that these sorts of pseudo-empirical exercises do not measure quality, only what teaching and learning experts consider to be quality, which is based on a very narrow band of indicators.

Clearly stung by students having referred to him as 'an arse-hole', Eric insisted that such evaluations:

> can't measure interaction, argument or the flow of dialogue that occurs in a tutorial or seminar. If the lecturer pushes the student, he can be labeled as aggressive or condescending – when in fact he is trying to encourage students to think, to develop as thinkers. So if the student says you're too pushy or whatever, this can, according to these sorts of survey instruments, indicate that you are a bad teacher. It's rubbish. The people who conduct these surveys fail to realise that education and learning are part of a process. Sometimes it involves

> discomfort and pain. I have students come back to me years later and say how much they appreciated being challenged and pushed, even though it felt uncomfortable at the time. But if you survey views at a moment in time, what does that tell you – that at that time the student felt this or that? Ultimately this sort of approach denies process.

For Eric, student evaluation practices are linked to corporate branding, in that appearance invariably triumphs over substance:

> [It's] the appearance of good education that counts. It's all very insidious, as academic careers are tied to this sort of process, and if you get bad feedback on your teaching it can prevent you getting promotion and you can be hounded by your head of school and teaching and learning people ... The risk-averse university can't have academics speaking out of turn or questioning the new orthodoxy because that will damage the brand.

Reducing the risk of students failing or dropping out is a top priority for most universities, particularly since much of their revenue depends on healthy retention rates. That's why – despite the fact that 20 per cent of undergraduate students never complete their courses – university administrators place such emphasis on learning and other systems of support.

Negative unit or course evaluations – or worse, direct student complaints – are greeted with great concern bordering on ritualised hysteria. Often accepted at face value, the academic against whom the complaint is lodged is duly chastised, set new goals and in some cases referred to teaching and learning experts for urgent ameliorative action. In really serious cases, if there are signs of confusion or life-threatening emotional instability, the subject may be referred to counsellors. In short, student evaluations can have significant effects on the academic, primarily because they privilege the views of student-shoppers who are the financial bedrock of the current marketised tertiary system.

But it's not all doom and gloom: for the academic, good evaluations can have distinct benefits, especially in terms of ensuring safe passage through performance planning exercises and in strengthening promotion applications. And there are few things more helpful in the latter regard than teaching awards.

And the award goes to ...

While negative results in student evaluations can have undeserved negative effects on an academic's career, positive results can prove something of a bonus – if again possibly undeserved. In an effort to promote excellence, bodies from all areas of tertiary education – from private providers to public institutions – now offer a dazzling array of teaching awards, perhaps reflecting our society's obsession with publicly rewarding supposedly notable achievers.

Before its axing by the Gillard government – ostensibly to pay for flood reconstruction in Queensland – the Australian Teaching and Learning Council spent a lot of its time and money handing out awards to worthy university lecturers. These included the Prime Minister's Award for Australian University Teacher of the Year; the annual Award for Teaching Excellence; Awards for Programs that Enhance Learning; the Career Achievement Award; and the Citation for Outstanding Contribution to Student Learning. Such commendations were not to be sniffed at: they came with significant financial rewards and the prospect of promotion on the back of accumulated evidence of nationally recognised teaching excellence.

But how reliable is the evidence upon which these and other awards are founded? The criteria differ markedly from one organisation to another, with some seeking to establish teaching prowess through a range of measures while others simply rely on input from minimal and not always reliable sources (usually students). Let's focus on those in-house awards that are handed out to academics in most of our universities. Typically, universities confer teaching awards in order to publicly acknowledge what they commonly refer to as 'excellence and innovation' in teaching. The process leading to an award requires the candidate to gain support and nominations from various parties, including colleagues, teaching and learning specialists, and students. An assessment panel made up of teaching and learning experts, pro vice chancellors, deans, heads of school, former award winners and so forth adjudicate the evidence and recommend which contender should be granted an award. Once conferred, teaching awards are often pinned by recipients on office doors, entered into CVs, announced at staff meetings and given prominence in promotion applications.

In one case, a colleague prepared the ground for eventual nomination for a teaching award by alerting a select group of students that an application was about to be submitted – and that therefore nominations would be warmly welcomed. The colleague was well known for delivering lectures full of entertaining gimmicks like over-elaborate Power Point presentations accompanied by an assortment of sound effects. As to the content of the lectures, the two I attended seemed rather lightweight and were based on scant and dated sources.

But in the world of teaching awards such things are often less important than the display of 'innovation' and 'student engagement', and evidence of positive 'learning outcomes'. The award in this case seems to have been based on criteria that elevated form over content and avoided reference as to whether anything significant had been taught in the unit. This is hardly surprising since the adjudication process dealt with the issue of content in the most general and ephemeral terms, preferring instead to emphasise student's vague and often ill-informed claims of teaching excellence and life-long learning.

In the case of the more prestigious NSW Quality Training Award – from one of the many state-level award authorities – the process of award assessment was perhaps a little more rigorous. It included assessment rituals like professional portfolios, observation of teaching, and interviews with colleagues, supervisors, students and others. Award aspirants were assessed on the basis of their ability to account for their approach to teaching in terms of knowledge foundations, and values and skills. Again it's hard to discern from the processes mentioned precisely how much emphasis was placed by adjudicators on the content and/or methodology of teaching, and how these should or could be disentangled in the assessment process. There is also the more practical question of who exactly is prepared to go through such a time-consuming exercise. Obviously some academics will subject themselves to such scrutiny – despite the huge amounts of time required to prepare applications. Many others, however, are either sceptical or cynical of the entire culture of teaching awards or have insufficient time or interest to nominate for such things.

These others may assert, with some justification, a wider concern: that awards are an integral part of a competitive and therefore ultimately divisive system that reflects the iniquitous values of a market-based economy. Moreover, the presentation of teaching awards to certain academics does not itself suggest that the recipients are inherently better educators than their colleagues. I know of some academics who are obsessed with obtaining teaching awards and go for them repeatedly, in some cases every year. Apart from the obvious benefits of prestige, possible promotion and so forth, there may be a deeper psychology at work here that harks back to the meritocratic system of glossy stars that were placed on one's academic work at primary school.

The fact is that teaching awards are no different from most others areas of life. They are subject to the same subjective judgments and intellectual preferences that characterise sports, film, music or arts prizes. Needless to say, there are – despite all the obstacles – some wonderful, dedicated educators in universities who inform, thrill and inspire their students and whose lectures remain lodged in students' mind long after graduation. Other educators can make use of all the technological pyrotechnics at their disposal and even deliver their material with gusto, but the message may simply fail to stick, or the performance depressingly outweighs intellectual content.

I recently asked some seasoned social science academics what they thought of teaching awards. The first, who had won several internal teaching awards and was keen observer of the tertiary scene, said that 'Teaching awards at universities are like death and taxes. Inevitable outcomes if you stick around long enough.' This is probably truer of some institutions than others.

A different view came from an associate professor with a particular interest in pedagogical matters. She recounted that 'I've heard the teaching awards referred to as rewarding "hobby farming" – they reward the most uncannily amateurish activities. You seem to get one if you do anything apart from teaching.' For her, 'hobby farming' meant engaging in the new catch-cry activities like 'innovation' (using new technical means of imparting information), 'student engagement' (getting students to undertake all manner of assessment items and encouraging them to communicate in groups) and 'achieving outcomes' (demonstrating through supposedly evidence-based research that students have actually learnt what is set out in the unit information guide). Many academics do indeed make a 'hobby' out of such activities, which usually implies that there is more attention to performance and less on the intellectual value of what is being taught.

Just tell me how to think

I want to emphasise again that, despite the above – no, make that *in spite* of the above – good, creative and rewarding teaching goes on across the university sector. I have often been amazed by the lengths to which university educators go to engage with their students and to make the educational experience an interesting and entertaining one. Yet at the same time there can be little doubt that the bureaucratic nature of modern university education has impacted significantly on the time and space that academics have to think about their teaching and to participate in an environment that is conducive to the best aspects of what, in the current vernacular is referred to as 'enlightened engagement'. The rigidification of tertiary teaching is an outgrowth of market-based, rationalist ways of thinking about 'service delivery', yet it is also a practice that carries with it the dangers of one-dimensional instrumentalism that binds academics to unit guides and which obsesses about learning outcomes and graduate attributes. Equally important, a system that is reliant on market-driven and career-focused education, with its roots in the productivist demands of the globalised capitalist economy, generates content more suited to job-readiness than anything approaching intelligent civic engagement. This is perhaps one reason why, as noted by Jen Rosenberg in the *Sydney Morning Herald*, many students – especially those in science and maths – question the relevance of their university education to their lives and communities.

To confront this orthodoxy is to be labelled a deviant or heretic, a relic of elitist higher education in a pre-branded era. To teach creatively, with gusto and wonder, but outside the remit of a standardised unit information guide – and irrespective of vocational and other concerns – is to put oneself at risk, particularly if students complain that they have not received 'value for money' or were not taught everything advertised in the unit information guide. Heretics are no longer burnt at the stake, but they can be held to account through rituals like performance management reviews.

Concern over how and what students are taught in today's universities has, however, come from some unexpected quarters, most recently from Professor Steven Schwartz, irrepressible about-to-retire vice chancellor of Macquarie University. Professor Schwartz has taken it upon himself to extol the virtues of 'practical wisdom' rather than the career-minded stuff that is currently imparted to job-hungry students. Professor Schwartz's advocacy of practical wisdom attracted a lot of public attention, not least because he personally volunteered to teach such a course to third-year students about to graduate. He declared that 'I don't want to teach students what to think. I want to teach them how to think.' He would teach wisdom relating to topical issues such as euthanasia, gay marriage and stem-cell cloning, and 'whether a Muslim cultural centre should be constructed near the Twin Towers site'. 'The purpose of the course', he intoned, was not to 'to finish the job of making our students wise, but to start it'.

In a bold assertion of his views in *On-Line Opinion* in July 2011, Professor Schwartz stated his objections to narrow, experienced-based university education. Instead, he argued that 'becoming wise requires not just having adventures but a cultured mind that is open, ready and able to absorb the lessons that experience teaches'. He further noted (absolutely rightly in my view) that 'life, death, love, beauty, courage, loyalty – all of these are omitted from our modern vocational curricula and yet, when it comes time to sum up our lives, they are the only things that ever really matter'.

'It is not easy', Professor Schwartz concluded with considerable understatement, 'for universities to go against the utilitarian flow, but it is our duty to try'.

Although stirring, Professor Schwartz's words are, I fear, likely to fall on deaf ears. Indeed, the hardened rationalists in Universities Australia, and policy advisers, are more likely to regard Professor Schwartz's views as quaint at best and deranged at worst. Personally, I think the brave professor should be commended, or perhaps given an award, for his outspokenness – even though I think he is articulating what amounts to a rather conservative view of liberal arts education grounded in abstract, de-contextualised ideas. But at least he has made an effort to break free from the shackles of one-eyed vocationalism. For that alone he deserves to be heard.

Yet after reading Professor Schwartz's views, one is left to ask – as did several commentators in our daily broadsheets – if students have not learnt wisdom by the third year of an undergraduate course at a major metropolitan university, then why on earth not? What does this say about the nature of education in the sector? How are we preparing students for later life? Even in those universities that do have more wide-ranging curricula – with many having core units on ethics, Indigenous Australia, communication, introductory politics and sociology, and in the case of Notre Dame university, reason and revelation and introductory philosophy – it is the values that underpin such offerings that really determine their ultimate worth.

Arguably, if a major role of the modern university is to act as a feeder for the economy and to produce job-ready students, then what is taught and learnt is shaped by such considerations. Unless wisdom is taught in the context of a more collectivised world-view, one that takes stock of one's location in the world and capacity to initiate change in accordance with certain values and principles, then university education is reduced to narrow individualistic pursuits. The demonstration of certain 'graduate attributes' – ethical understanding, critical reflection, intellectual rigour, cultural awareness – thus end up as commodified artefacts in a student portfolio, platitudes to be presented to a prospective employer rather than a statement of commitment to active citizenship and community involvement. In short, 'wisdom' is more than a simple imparting of itemised knowledge. It should indeed include, as Professor Schwartz has suggested, teaching students how to think, but – and this is an important rider – it should be underpinned by socially relevant and civically minded values that enable us to become historically and globally aware, active citizens.

But just try putting all that in a course proposal and getting it through the curriculum committee without the usual rigidified claptrap. Try suggesting that the standardisation of curricula and vocationally obsessed education are intellectually stultifying. The fact is that the practice of teaching in Australian and most Western universities reflects a corporatised ethos that cuts across various industrial and commercial sectors but which ultimately helps feed economic growth, GDP, capital accumulation, profit, whatever – end games in the context of current global crises that are rightly coming under close and increasingly critical scrutiny!

5

Research, metrics and money

What passes for research in my neck of the woods is trying to cram your reading and writing into the odd free moments between doing everything else. There really isn't time to sit and think in this job. Funny that, eh? I'm supposed to be an academic.

SENIOR LECTURER IN CRIMINOLOGY, QUEENSLAND

Trying to get everyone to produce research to some sort of 'world standard' – whatever that means – is destined to be an absolutely ludicrous, lamentable failure.

GARETH EVANS, CHANCELLOR OF THE AUSTRALIAN NATIONAL UNIVERSITY

Since the mid-1990s I have come to understand that academic life in today's university system is largely about toeing the corporate line so that the process of producing higher education and other related outputs can continue unhindered. The more I have looked at the internal workings of the system, the more I have realised that almost everything that takes place in our tertiary institutions can be sheeted home to the bottom line of income-generation.

Although it is possible to resist this sort of pressure (see chapter 7), academics only do so at great personal and professional risk: denial of promotion, constant badgering and bullying by performance-obsessed administrators, and regular reminders of your conditions of service by officious human resources personnel. But deep in the academic soul – and this excludes many 'para-academics' who often seem bereft of such spirit – there is a yearning to do research and scholarship in areas that matter personally, professionally and politically. Unfortunately, the rationalist ideologues, bean-counters, time-and-motion supervisors and performance checkers now run universities, meaning that the ever-diminishing chances of doing worthwhile research have been increasingly side-lined by the drudgery of having to make money. True, universities continue to do a lot of very useful research that is conducive to the common good. But it is also the case that the system generally encourages such activity because it brings in the dollars, large chunks of which, by the way, end up in 'central' or faculty funds rather than in the hands of worthy researchers.

This preoccupation with income-generation is most apparent when it comes to research-related matters. Typically, what an academic chooses to research is less important from an institutional standpoint than obtaining a grant and the funds that the university can derive from this. Money concerns are also evident when academics attend preparatory meetings to discuss how grant applications should be formulated. I have attended such meetings and, again, minimal attention is given to the intellectual content or social purpose of the research. Rather, the focus is on how to tweak the application so that it has the best chance of being approved. By the same token, promotions committees are usually not so much interested in what contribution an academic's research may have made to society as they are in the fact that candidates have secured research grants.

Faced with such instrumental concerns, most academics, I am sad to say, hunker down and simply 'play the game'. For some it can be a dispiriting experience to realise that your worth as an academic is tied so closely to values that privilege money-making over intellectual content and/or the collective good. You begin to feel like the proverbial cog in a giant corporate machine. As I suggested in the Introduction, academics' submission to the new order has led to a kind of zombification of university life in which scholars shuffle dolefully around campuses like the incarcerated Billy Hayes in *Midnight Express*. They often undertake particular sorts of research and other activities because the corporate system requires this of them and because each institution is compelled to strive for a place in the competitive market. All that is left, as far as administrators are concerned, is to make sure that 'mechanisms' are put in place to 'encourage' research, and then to make sure that the activities of academics are closely monitored and regularly reviewed to make sure they produce measurable 'output'. That said, 'good', socially useful and life-enhancing research goes on in universities – but these days it rarely strays very far from considerations of the cash nexus.

My concern in this chapter is with how research and scholarship are experienced by academics across various institutions and disciplines – recognising that great divisions exist in this regard – and how the pursuit of 'quality' and income-generation have inflicted lasting damage on these vitally important activities. But first some reflections on academics' experiences of attempting to do research in today's higher education institutions.

Knowledge crunching

As with most other activities, research and scholarship in universities are usually crammed into temporal slots outside the more regular and onerous demands of teaching and administration – unless, that is, you are lucky enough to be granted study leave, obtain a research position, buy your way out of teaching, or are employed at one of the elite universities. For most academics, however, research and scholarship are allocated various blocks of time under the workload formula, with most allocations hovering somewhere between a quarter to a third of total load. As noted in the next chapter, the reality is not as neat and tidy as such allocations might suggest. Let me offer a brief personal example of the problems that beset attempts to calibrate research and scholarship activities.

A few years ago, I began preparing an article for a well-known and highly regarded education journal. I was attempting a critical overview of the post-9/11 academic literature (mainly in the area of political science) which, as you can imagine, involved an abundance of reading. All in all, the research took me a good six months of thinking, reading, talking with colleagues and eventually, drafting and re-drafting the manuscript. The resulting article (or 'outcome' in the current vernacular) received very positive reviews and was published shortly thereafter. Prior to all this, I had tried to negotiate adequate time to prepare the article with my then head of school. She pronounced that the article could only be counted as 'one unit', and therefore was to be allocated only a small amount of preparatory hours. (I can't recall how many exactly, but certainly less than three days worth.) I asked a provocative question: 'How long do you think this one unit will take me to complete?'

'No idea', she replied with unintended modesty.

I gave her the low-down, but all she could do was mumble something about the spread of my professional responsibilities and my 'excessive' focus on research and scholarship activities to the apparent exclusion of everything else. I was annoyed with myself for having engaged the issue, since I had resolved to always try and ignore all workload deliberations, however irritating they might be. In a very short time it became horribly obvious to me that the application of the workload formula and resulting allocation of time for research and scholarship were as subjective, and therefore malleable and inaccurate, as they possibly could be.

To get a clearer idea of how the workload formula works in relation to research matters, I spoke with an experienced official from the National Tertiary Education Union. He stated that the rule of thumb for workload distribution in the standard formula went something like this: teaching 60 per cent, research 30 per cent, and community engagement/professional service 10 per cent. Apparently this allocation was broadly accepted by most universities. 'It's all bollocks though', he admitted:

> What's down on paper and what happens in reality are of course two different things. Most academics at lecturer levels are treated like cart-horses. They can be given up to 75 per cent teaching, with 15 per cent or less for research. It's a joke of course. And if you're a casual then it gets worse. You can end up in with practically no research allocation – as most do.

Worried about the implications of all this, I approached the research folk at the NTEU headquarters in Melbourne. 'Have you got any data on academic workload allocations in Australian universities?', I asked.

'No', came the terse reply. 'Try the University of Western Sydney. I think their NTEU people did a study on this.'

My NTEU contact was kind enough to send me a copy of the union's report, *Overload: The role of work role escalation and micro-management of work patterns in loss of morale and collegiality at UWS*. The title alone tells you all you need to know about the goings on at UWS circa 2009: a litany of academic complaints familiar throughout the university sector. As a result of financial difficulties during the 1990s, UWS management had decided to embark on a programme of radical 'restructuring' – a euphemism for staff cuts and increased workloads. The shedding of academic positions through voluntary and other redundancies meant a cranking up of teaching and allied duties – and of course, a winding back of research time for the remaining academics. But that was only part of the problem. According to *Overload*:

> The intensity of teaching in a university with arguably Australia's highest staff–student ratio is exacerbated by far-flung campuses, severe parking problems, large cohorts with specific educational needs, and ever-changing armies of casual academics, often post-graduate students, that have replaced collegial teaching teams from which academics previously drew support, as well as the loss of administrative support. All of these issues are intrinsic to the economic pressures of a relatively young university that needed rapid growth to assure its place in the sector.

Because of a lack of transparency by UWS management in relation to the real amount of work undertaken under the annual allocation of 1725 hours, academics found themselves hugely over-burdened and unable to cope with work demands. Worse, according to the report, was that the actual level of work had been 'lost in complex interpretations and new school policies that impose rigidity, micro-management and hyper-vigilance, because of the need for economy in educating larger cohorts'.

In a management sleight of hand common across the higher education sector, many aspects of work at UWS were conveniently omitted in workload calculations. *Overload* recorded that such omissions included:

> coordination of small units and those in which the coordinator does not teach some lectures, and the actual time it takes to mark assessments when compared to what is 'allowed'. Real work, time-hungry tasks, such as administration and travelling between campuses, are encapsulated in unrealistic time budgets.

Using an array of research methods – surveys, focus groups and the like – the NTEU study noted that the majority of the full-time UWS academics surveyed routinely exceeded their allocated 37.5 hours per week, with over half working from 8 am to 8 pm, five days a week. Almost 100 per cent said they regularly exceeded the weekly allocation over the course of a year. Not surprisingly, most academics reported they were overworked, burnt out, not coping, running out of energy, stressed out, not sleeping, and plain knackered. Doing research and scholarship in such an environment proved very difficult of course, with most academics simply trying to keep on top of their routine administrative and teaching responsibilities.

The combination of rising staff–student ratios, continual small- and large-scale restructuring, micro-management and highly suspect workload formulae have made it very difficult (impossible perhaps?)

for academics to manage their time within the given allocations. One of the first things to fall off the trolley is research. True, UWS is an extreme case but – if my own encounters with academics are anything to go by – the same hazardous workload practices occur throughout the university sector. Between attending to multifarious student demands, form-filling and committee attendance, research is something that is jammed into occasional 'spare' hours when academics are usually too exhausted to do anything. As one UWS academic quoted in *Overload* remarked: 'there is a lot of pressure to do more with less time. The system is not working or helping anyone. Someone needs to realise that you cannot go on like this forever.'

Such cries in the dark have come from all levels of academic staff at UWS and will undoubtedly register with others across the higher education sector. As one social sciences lecturer in Adelaide told me:

> research is something you do when you can. The idea that you sit around smoking a pipe and contemplating existence and that sort of thing is utter crap. The modern university, God help us, is all about motion and measuring motion. The workload formula might allocate this or that to research, but just try doing it. I can't think when I last had time to read, write and reflect. I hang out for study leave, but the process of getting there with all the form-filling and so on takes up even more time. The whole thing really is quite insane.

The 'typical' week

Levels of workload obviously vary from one institution to another. But what might a 'typical' week look like for, say, a lecturer in humanities? How much research and scholarship can they squeeze into a 37.5 hour week? The first thing to consider is that many school heads will tell their charges that you do your real research and scholarly work at the weekends or in the evenings – that's just part and parcel of being an academic, or so we're told. This sort of patronising advice might have worked a few years ago, but these days it is likely to send a feisty academic straight to his or her union representative and then to an industrial tribunal. And with good reason.

The fact is that many academics feel exploited in a system that demands more than the working week can deliver. I spoke about this with a lecturer in arts in Sydney. Although not the sort of person to blow a fuse too easily, I could nonetheless see the veins on the side of her head pulsating as she related the challenges of trying to do research in a hyperactive environment:

> I usually do a heap of work over the weekend like answering emails – mainly from students and catching up with all the stuff I couldn't get to through the week. The inquiries from students are endless, there's no reprieve.
>
> By the time Monday comes around you feel as if you've already done a week's worth of work. Then you're back in the office, the phone starts, or an administrator comes in asking you to fill in a form.
>
> Then a student might knock on your door. He's upset because he can't cope or doesn't like his grade, or doesn't understand the assignment question even though there are pages of guide notes. You're tempted to ask whether this can wait until the formal consultation time on Wednesday. No it can't.

I was about to ask a question about student contact but my interviewee was rapidly on to another issue:

In between such occurrences you have to begin preparing for teaching, there's photocopying to do but the machine isn't working, and there's a queue. The head of school passes your room and has a brief chat, as does anyone else with a burning issue. You're just about to start on some reading but there's another knock on the door. It's the rep from the publishing company in Melbourne. You'd like to tell him to piss off as he's smarmy but you know you'll get a free textbook out of him – and in any case, you've lodged a manuscript with the company so you don't want to cheese anyone off. You finish with him. Peace at last.

But wait, there's a crisis. Someone from teaching and learning wants to talk with you about an urgent matter. Not them again! If it wasn't for them I wouldn't have been landed with four assessment items which make my workload impossible. I should never have agreed to see them. Simon sticks his head around the door. 'Are you going to the staff meeting?'

Again, I tried to interject, without success.

'Oh shit', I think, 'I haven't got time'. I urgently scour the minutes of the previous meeting to try and locate the action items that relate to me. Oh Christ! I'll just have to make something up and/or that the data wasn't available or that I was sick. It's 4 pm by the time the wretched meeting finishes and here I am with all this work to do. Never mind. Friday is my allocated research day.

Friday comes around and I am grappling with my study leave application, and essays that I haven't yet marked, and the chapter of someone's PhD that has been sitting on my desk for weeks. The emails flow in and there are students

> complaining on the on-line discussion board. I have to start preparing for next week's lecture. The tutor has gone sick and I need to get a replacement ... Do you get the picture?

Crystal clear.

'Is there anything like a normal week? Does such a thing exist? And how can you do research and scholarship in this environment?', I asked. She looked at me as if I were ET.

> Get real, Richard.
>
> There's no such thing as a normal day, let alone week, and there's never a place where you can hide to do research. Most academics I know don't have time to do any reading, let alone thinking. The imperative is to be constantly active, which means that we don't get time to think. Very little time is allocated for research work and it's never ever enough. They load you up with nonsense hours and expect the world.
>
> Research often feels like a bit of a luxury.

The worst thing you could say to this frustrated academic is that she needs to improve her time management skills. This is likely to generate thoughts of immanent violence. The other advice might be simply to shut out all the interruptions and proceed headlong with research and scholarship. This might work in a sympathetic school environment, or if you have a formidable track record of grants and publications. Only then might you be lucky enough to be left alone.

One senior academic in social work at an elite Melbourne university was in this category. Describing himself as 'selfish', he had carved out a safe and comfortable space by simply obsessing about researching, publishing and acquiring a lucrative ARC grant. I asked him how he approached research work:

> Doing research? Look, it's different for everyone. It depends on which university or school you're in, your head of school and your own priorities. I suppose I am lucky in that I work at a G8 university that really wants us to be productive in terms of gaining grants and publishing – that suits me. I have a good track record and am at a senior level, so by and large, I am left to get on with things. If you have a good track record you get left alone.

'What about admin? Does that affect your work?'

> Well it does, and there is a lot of it. There are always things to deal with like student complaints and related problems, but some of my colleagues take a more therapeutic approach than I would and that takes up their time. A lot of people get caught up in process rather than outcomes.

'What do you mean by "therapeutic"?', I asked.

'You know – the sort of academic who gets bogged down with a student's psychological or learning problems. That's not their job.'

So, the preferred logic here appeared to be: focus on what you're meant to be doing as an academic and let specialists deal with the tricky personal problems of students. The problem, of course, is that so befuddled are academics by the multiple demands of the daily grind and the related pressure of performance goals that it's not easy to off-load unwanted work demands. As Annie, a law lecturer from one of Brisbane's smaller universities remarked: 'I can barely keep my head above water. I'm not sure what my job is any longer. I'm not sure what it means to be an academic these days. We're too concerned with meeting performance goals.' Despite such hindrances, a lot of academics do try to get on the research treadmill, including heroic attempts to 'land' a career-enhancing grant.

The grants lottery

Another disgruntled academic, this time in the field of business and commerce, remarked:

> I'm an associate professor and all I do is churn out grant applications because that's what the university expects me to do. I help generate income for the university, that's my job. And it's murder. You can spend months on an application only for it to fall flat on its face at the last hurdle. I don't get time to do the actual research as I'm always applying for funds so that I can do research!

Complaints about the competitive nature of the grant application process – privileging more seasoned academics and the elite universities – were legion among my respondents. 'I don't even bother these days', said one security and intelligence expert. 'It's too hard, too competitive and time consuming. I've got better things to do with my life.'

The success rates for Australian Research Council 'discovery' grants (focused on funding and promoting basic and applied research for the 'knowledge economy') hover around 23 per cent across disciplines, over 44 per cent for 'linkage' grants (focusing on 'long term strategic research alliances' and international 'partnerships'), and 15 per cent for early career researcher grants (for the 'best and brightest'). It is hardly surprising that academics choose less hazardous routes to scholarship. Whichever way you look at it, the fact is that 75 per cent of discovery, over 50 per cent of linkage and a staggering 85 per cent of early career researcher grant applications are unsuccessful. At the very least, this suggests a very modest return on academics' investment of time, energy and resources. Given that these applications can take weeks or even months to complete, and involve considerable cerebral effort and engagement with various advisors and administrators, the energy expended on a failed bid often feels like a colossal waste of time and money. To be sure, many applicants will resubmit to the same or other grant bodies, but only a small number of scholars – most often in the natural sciences – will succeed in obtaining grants.

The latter point is borne out in research conducted by Professor Emeritus Frank Larkins for the LH Martin Institute at the University of Melbourne. Drawing on ARC data and various measurement instruments, Professor Larkins notes that science-based disciplines produce more research 'outputs' (including grant acquisitions) than the arts, humanities and social sciences. This varies from university to university, although the more established elite institutions perform consistently better across all disciplines than their newer counterparts, especially in the natural sciences. Part of the explanation for this is to do with the more 'established' research cultures operating in natural sciences and the emphasis placed by the government on the creation of a competitive knowledge economy. But it is also due to the greater funding from industry flowing into the sciences, mainly for 'innovation' purposes. Professor Larkins adds that:

> Many of the more recently established unaligned universities have a lower level of research discipline activity, principally researching in fewer science and technology disciplines. This is not surprising given the high cost of research infrastructure required by many science-based disciplines to undertake world standard research.

All this points to the fact that some universities do more research than others, and that those academics in the more 'liberal' disciplines have comparatively less access to research funds. Most arts, humanities and social science academics therefore will plod along using their own resources, derived from faculty or school funds (if there are any) and income gained from consultancies (which are hard to obtain). Some universities run small internal grant schemes for early career researchers, and there are even occasional 'seeding funds' for those seeking to develop especially complex grant applications. But for most academics, money for research is as scarce as hen's teeth. And even if you are lucky enough to obtain a grant, there may not be the time to do the actual research. As one senior social scientist in Queensland observed: 'I got an ARC research grant a few years back and it was the worst thing that ever happened to me. I just couldn't get to the work. There were so many other things to do. It was a nightmare.'

Few if any of my respondents liked completing research grant applications: it was the intellectual equivalent to water-boarding. Dennis, a sociologist from Queensland, remarked that 'writing grants is torture. On most occasions you get the flick. It's only recently that our school has allocated hours that recognise the effort you might put into a failed application. Before then you got nothing.'

'Sounds a bit soul destroying', I observed.

'It is. The thing is that everyone is going for grants these days. We're like rats on a wheel. It's so damn competitive. You put in all that effort and you get knocked back. There must be more to life than that.'

'So', I inquired, 'how do you go about your research? Isn't that one of your core areas of work?'

Dennis returned to the familiar theme of busyness:

> Mate, universities don't create the environment for research. We're teaching our arses off and doing stacks of administra-

> tion and that sort of shit. The first thing that falls off the table is research. If you want to do research you have to work seven days a week and a lot of us don't want to do that. There's such an emphasis on teaching and supporting students through the learning process that we haven't got time to do research. The administration side of things has gotten completely out of hand. I've just come out of a meeting where we've discussed moderation and peer review reports, which are things recently added to our admin load. Management keeps piling on more and more things. The only way you can get to your research is if you have a brutal mentality and shut the door on everything, including ad hoc student inquiries and crises that arise on a daily basis.

The notion of a 'brutal mentality' is not too far removed from the Melbourne academic who earlier talked about being selfish. Perhaps that's the trick: ignore all the demands and get on with what you want to do. But, as a West Australian academic lamented, 'You have to have a pretty thick skin though, because we have a lot of needy students out here'.

Despite such views, and despite their being only a minority of applicants, some academics are successful at obtaining research grants. They wade through the lengthy application forms – which demand copious amounts of intellectual justification and highly detailed information, including the dreaded budget – during periods of study leave or on top of everything else they do. These people demand our respect – although one would also expect premature aging to set in as a result of their considerable efforts.

Many universities celebrate successful grant applications by broadcasting the news on their websites. For example, Queensland University of Technology – not an institution known for its humility

– lists its ARC linkage grantees by discipline through its Office of Research and via a carefully crafted website – a practice similar to most other Australian universities. The point about such lists is that they are meant not simply to celebrate successful grant application but are also part of a marketing strategy aimed at extolling the scholastic virtues of each institution. Then the university can crow about 'innovation', 'best practice' and 'international competiveness' and other tags that make up the corporate brand. Thus, successful grant applications fulfill a number of very important aims both for the academic (prestige, promotion) and the institution (reputation, market appeal and public acknowledgment of 'research output' – not to mention basic revenue). As far as the academic is concerned, universities will give you, and forgive you, anything as long as the money keeps rolling in. Few if any universities will now promote people who do not obtain research grants. Academics know the score when they submit applications to the big providers like the ARC: career prospects can be transformed by a successful bid. This is why, when the letter of confirmation or rejection finally arrives in the post, screams of delight or howls of anguish can be heard down the corridor. I have seen perfectly sane individuals run up and down hallways waving letters and shouting 'I got it! I got it!' while those who miss out shuffle along like long-term prison inmates. Relationships may lie in ruins, wrinkles deepened, but what the hell – it was worth it, wasn't it?

For those mere mortals left behind in the routine drudgery of academic life, the world suddenly seems a very bleak place indeed. Numerous thoughts cross one's mind. Perhaps I should put in an application? Does it really matter? If he or she can do it, surely I can? The sad fact is that most academics miss out on the joys of successful grant applications. This may not be altogether disastrous. As noted below, many universities seem less than interested in research anyway, or perhaps academics simply haven't the time, inclination or resources to carry out such work. Or – more likely – they just can't compete with the more prestigious universities which are, in any event, better at attracting and sometimes 'poaching' scholars with good grant acquisition records.

The great ERA delusion

Presided over by the Australian Research Council, the trendy-sounding Excellence in Research for Australia (ERA) is the federal government's latest attempt at measuring academic research quality and highlighting shortcomings among the supposedly non-productive universities. Hinged on the highly suspect proposition that research outputs and impacts can indeed be measured, the ERA stands as a testament to a positivistic culture that seems determined to subject under-achieving academics and institutions to an ugly round of public humiliation. So far, it has succeeded – but it has also brought with it all manner of unintended consequences.

For the aficionado of empirical method – and its associated paraphernalia of tables, histograms and pie charts – the *Excellence in Research Australia National Report* of 2010 makes for astonishing reading. It begins with Senator Kim Carr, the then federal Minister for Innovation, Industry, Science and Research, lauding this resplendent piece of organisational research. ERA, he boasts:

> is the culmination of the Australian Labor Government's bold endeavour to develop a transparent and workable system to assess the quality of research in Australia. It provides a comprehensive overview of the quality of research undertaken in higher education institutions across the country in an international context.

Boldness is certainly a hallmark of the report, which sets out the intricate methodologies and results of a mammoth empirical exercise that allows ERA to compare the research outputs of Australian with overseas universities and lay the ground for government investment in research initiatives.

First of all, ERA divides the entire research spectrum in Australia into 'discipline clusters': Physical, Chemical and Earth Sciences; Humanities and Creative Arts; Engineering and Environmental Sciences; Social, Behavioural and Economic Sciences; Mathematical, Information and Computing Sciences; Biological Sciences and Biotechnology; Biomedical and Clinical Health Sciences; and Public and Allied Health Sciences. These form the foundations of its ranking system, in which various indicators are used to assess research quality, volume and activity, application and recognition (or 'esteem'). For example, ERA assesses research quality using measures like peer review and citation analyses, while it calculates research application according to commercialisation, income and other applied indices. The actual process of assessment was undertaken by a number of Research Evaluation Committees made up of 149 'distinguished and internationally recognised researchers' with 'expertise' in research evaluation. To compare and contrast quality, output, application and recognition, the committees employed a complex array of benchmarking techniques that allowed for national and international comparisons to be made.

The resulting aggregated ratings – pounced on instantly by eagle-eyed university managers – compared each university according to discipline clusters, which were then set against an aggregated world standard. Universities were thus placed above, at, or below this standard. Many of the usual suspects – ANU, the University of Melbourne, the University of Queensland, UNSW, the University of Sydney, the University of Western Australia and Monash University

– figured in the top ten. Even QUT and Macquarie University made unexpected appearances in this elite grouping. Languishing somewhere near the foot of the rankings were poor old Southern Cross University, the University of Ballarat, the University of the Sunshine Coast, the University of Central Queensland and the Northern Territory's Batchelor College. At least nine universities were deemed under the world standard, while half a dozen institutions could only be assessed for a paltry number of research activities, which – according to *The Australian*'s 'Higher Education' supplement – raises the question of 'what it means to be a comprehensive university'.

Well, what it certainly does mean is that quite a few universities are doing precious little research and, as a result, are failing to integrate their research and teaching practices – one of the principal characteristics of a functioning higher education institution. Considerable concern has been expressed in relation to the fact that, according to the ERA results, the physical, biological and medical sciences did rather well whereas there was 'poor performance across the board in arts, humanities and social sciences'.

The reasons for such disparities are of course complex, but are linked to the cultures of research and publishing that exist in the sciences, and the comparative scarcity of both grants and publication outlets for the rest. Either way, the ERA results have given ammunition to those who think that the arts, humanities and social sciences are less worthwhile than the more solid and established 'natural sciences'. The ERA rankings have also led to even more public discussion on the proposed creation of 'teaching only' universities – a tacit admission that some universities cannot or will not encourage their academics to do research.

The Australian was particularly scathing about the skewed results emanating from the ERA: 'It has laid bare the myths of research excellence spun by most marketing departments in most universities, revealing that better than world class is, on average, something only a dozen universities can lay claim to'. But, it added almost as an afterthought, 'there are pockets of excellence throughout'.

This last point is important to bear in mind, as it is too easy to slam certain universities for under-performing on the research front. By dint of reputation and better resources, the elite universities can attract more grants and are often able to poach 'research active' scholars. Also, newer universities tend to specialise in innovative and developing areas of study, while regional universities may not have the cultural emphasis on research that exists in more established metropolitan institutions. But, as Gavin Moodie has rightly observed, 'It is neither in the national nor students' interest to have large numbers studying in apparent research wastelands'. Ultimately, these wasteland universities may have to pay a heavy price for their lack of research output, although the exact ramifications – especially in terms of loss of funding – are as yet unknown.

Quantifying quality: The journals ranking fiasco

My brief overview of the empirical measurement juggernaut cannot do justice to the overarching complexities revealed in its *National Report*. Only a person steeped in obsessive empirical method – and with the patience of a saint – could begin to navigate through this positivist thicket. Yet it is worth scrutinising one key area used to assess research performance – journal articles – as a way of revealing the banality of the ERA's approach. Before its axing by Minister Carr in May 2011, the system that ERA used to rank academic journals stood as the highpoint of what one of my former academic colleagues referred to as 'empirical lunacy'.

Not surprisingly, making sense of the complex empirical apparatus used to assess something as varied as the field of academic and professional journals was always likely to prove difficult. The report in which the first ranking appeared told its readers to refer back to the ERA website for further information on the guidelines and methods housed under the System to Evaluate the Excellence of Research (SEER). Obediently, I ventured forth to find myself immersed in a website of bewildering complexity. The list of journals covered by the ERA metric specialists ran to a staggering 20 000 publications from around the world. The formidable catalogue makes for entertaining reading. Take the following journals, which ERA ranked from the lofty A* to basement C:

Liver International (A*)
Journal of Transcultural Nursing (A*)
Journal of the Study of Jewish Mythical Texts (A*)
Journal of Theological Interpretation (A)
Pacific Performance Paradigm (A)
Sexually Transmitted Infections (B)
Polish Polar Research (C)
Journal of the Greater Houston Dental Society (C)
Mining History (C)
Journal of the Brazilian Computer Society (C)
Journal of the European Pentecostal Association (C)
Journal of the Virtual Explorer (C)
Soap and Cosmetics (C).

Quite why these journals were so ranked was something of a mystery. Additionally, some odd developments occurred in the wake of this ranking exercise. For instance, the reputable journal *People and Place*, which for 18 years pumped out high-quality peer-reviewed articles on various social issues, was initially ranked B. Later, for some strange reason, it was relegated to C. Since then, with its funds pulled by its sponsor, Monash University, the journal has gone out of business – and with it an important resource for countless numbers of scholars. Also, as many academic observers have noted, to have privileged international journals well ahead of most Australian outlets, and to have ranked *People and Place* alongside *Soap and Cosmetics* and the *Journal of the European Pentecostal Association*, appeared both arbitrary and high-handed.

Predictably, the ERA journal-ranking system seriously annoyed a lot of academics, and not simply because what Professor Douglas Kirsner of Deakin University described as its 'aura of false objectivity'. It also ignored the fact that some disciplines produced more journals than others, and were therefore likely to have more articles published in journals ranked A* and A. By the same token, the spread of journals across the rankings also varied wildly across disciplines. For instance, only 8 per cent of zoology journals were ranked A* or A, while in historical studies it was around 30 per cent. Additionally, it was not clear why certain journals were ranked as they had been, and various professional associations grappled with the ERA to get their journals re-ranked.

These sorts of reactions were only part of a more general assault on the ERA, which is now seen by many academics as part of a stifling empirical enterprise devoted to measuring scholarly activity under the pretext of 'quality assurance'. Like hospitals and schools, universities have been increasingly subjected to scrutiny on the grounds of 'openness' and 'accountability' – although the real agenda, according to Simon Cooper and Anna Poletti, is the disciplining of academics so that they perform their duties in accordance with the demands of the prevailing neo-liberal order. In addition to questioning the ERA's over-reliance on journals as a measure of something called 'quality', Cooper and Poletti note that it also ignored the rise of online scholarship and the many alternative approaches to pedagogical engagement, and relied too readily on questionable processes of peer review. Simon and Poletti make this vital point:

> Privileging journal ranking as an indication of quality fails to comprehend how academics work within a contemporary context, how they work as individuals and as colleagues, how they co-operate across national and disciplinary borders, and how they research within a digital culture that is well on the way to displacing paper-based academic publishing.

They might have added that the total disregard of anything to do with content says a lot about the general trajectory of the ERA's concerns. In fact, the more one scrutinises the ERA project the more it begins to sound and feel like an anti-intellectual exercise; more accounting than accountability. Whatever else it claims to do, the ERA system certainly takes the fun out of research. As social work academic Max Travers from the University of Tasmania observes: 'the fact that we have established a system in which *where* you publish is more important than *what* you publish seems to reinforce the tendency to produce uninteresting work'.

It would, however, be silly to ignore the damaging effects of the ERA ranking system on academic life. This system has profoundly impacted upon the culture of academic research and publishing, and therefore upon how scholarship is conducted. Here are a few pointers as to how this has occurred. First, from a senior humanities academic in South Australia:

> Look, there's no doubt that the journal-ranking system has had a huge impact on how we carry out our work. Even though it has since been abolished, it has left the sector in a mess. When I was appointed, it was noted in my contract that

> I should publish annually in A or A* journals. The problem is that journals get re-classified all the time, so you spend your time writing an article believing it is an A-ranking journal, only to find it has been downgraded. The opposite happens too. For example, I was fortunate enough when I applied for my job that some of my main publications were re-classified from C to A. That counted for a lot and perhaps got me over the line. Careers can be made or broken by this stuff, yet there is a certain arbitrariness and unpredictability about the whole process.

The same academic talked about his strategy for engaging various audiences in relation to both his professional concerns and workload requirements:

> I write for a professional audience so I have to strike a balance between writing for those audiences even though these publications may get a low ranking. I also write other articles specifically so that I can get some professional kudos. The problem of course is that in my discipline there are very few highly regarded journals – maybe there's one. We can't all get in there.

A lecturer in business and tourism in Western Australia was a little more acerbic in his views on the ERA:

> The problem with the ERA is that it has no capacity of distinguishing between early career researchers and those academics at professorial levels who have a track record. They're treated the same, which is fucking ridiculous. I mean, there is a slight advantage for scholars who have been in the system for some time. It's not a level playing field, is it?'

The ERA legacy

In one month in early 2011, largely in reaction to the sort of empirical arbitrariness that seemed to prevail in the journals-ranking system, the ERA received over 6800 submissions from academics, editors and various professional associations – a startling number that overwhelmed administrators at the ARC central office. Faced with such extensive criticism, the journals-ranking project was axed: a terrible humiliation for the ARC and the responsible minister, and a colossal waste of time and money. Although the ranking system now lies in ruins, many academics I spoke to felt that the legacy of a publications hierarchy will endure for years to come. 'That's how we now think', said one political scientist from Brisbane:

> There was a time when you'd write for a number of audiences rather than being governed by the rankings set by some amorphous group of assessors. It's so limiting to our profession. How are we meant to be public intellectuals if we write for journals that no-one ever reads?

One of the most visceral reactions to the ranking of journals was in relation to the promotions process. Many academics I talked to felt, at the time of the ranking and thereafter, that promotion panels look differently at what is on an applicant's publications list. One Melbourne academic commented that 'the fact is that managers look at journals through the prism of ranking, and they expect to see academics publish in what they consider to be reputable journals'. Similarly, an NTEU representative noted the many complaints which he had received from those who had missed out on promotion as a result of the journal rankings:

> When the journal ranking came out, management used the

> rankings to consider promotion applications ... So the failure rate, in terms of the last promotion round, went up by two-thirds – mainly because of the ERA publications expectations ... The ERA criteria were used as a justification for knocking people back when this wasn't said to the candidates when they first considered applying for promotion. The criteria were entirely altered ... the damage has been done. The mind-set of those who sit on promotion panels has been altered. They now look for certain journals that were ranked at A or A* at the time of the ERA exercise. That's where their mind-sets are.

Another point raised by my irate respondent related to the growing tendency of universities, in the wake of the journal rankings jamboree, to recruit high-achieving academics, especially those who can churn our 'prestigious' journal articles: 'There was a mad rush here to sign on people with loads of ranked journals so that the university could be bumped up the ranking scale. We were right down the bottom end of publications output, so people here were desperate.'

As a prolific writer himself, this academic identified yet another problem that impacted both journal editors and academics around the country – the stampede of submissions of articles to the more highly ranked journals:

> Ranked journals were being flooded with submissions. It was bizarre! One of the hospitality journals which has an A ranking used to get 300 or so submissions a year. Then it went up to about 1500. And of course there was a bottleneck and most people producing great articles probably couldn't get in, or if they did it was likely to be in five years time when the stuff is completely out of date. There's always been a bit of a hierarchy in the journal scene but the ERA has reinforced that many times over.

Since the abolition of the journal rankings system in early 2011, academics have found themselves adrift, with no real idea whether a different version of the system is to be wheeled out, or whether it will be permanently set aside. What we do know is that, as a result of the introduction of the ranking system, universities like Murdoch and La Trobe have already altered their entire approach to research and scholarship, relying heavily on the calibrated approach to research outputs adopted by the ERA. At the very least, the legacy of the ERA project has been, according to Professor Douglas Kirsner at Deakin University, 'to second guess the government's next moves' and to fall into place in anticipation.

With the benefit of experience, the ERA now looks increasingly like a questionable empirical exercise. The entire logic of the ERA project has been subject to widespread criticism (and ridicule) on the grounds that attempts to quantify and measure research and scholarship are bound to run into trouble. Quite simply, if a first-year sociology student were confronted with the proposition that it is possible to objectively measure and rank scholarly publications or to rank other research outputs, then she or he – if properly educated – would surely have a critical field day. The very first thing he or she might do would be to unpack the flawed assumptions contained in the ERA bag of tricks – the main one being that ranking makes little sense in the context of the very different contexts in which individuals, universities and research disciplines operate. The use of a standard measure to assess 'outputs' or 'quality', irrespective of these differences, means that the results simply reflect the logic of the standard measure that you started with. It's the classic positivist fallacy that something out there – in this case 'quality' – exists to be measured, when in fact it only 'exists' because the empiricists insist it does according to their methodological parameters. No wonder the feisty editor of the *Journal of Higher Education Policy and Management*, Ian

Dobson, remarked that 'ERA rankings have more holes than a crumpet ... the whole process is an operational shambles that depends on a lot of people spending a lot of time counting and lobbying'.

Only part of the problem

As irony would have it, I met up with three Queensland law academics in a trendy, down-town Brisbane bistro called 'Era'. We chatted about the ARC's questionable quest for quality. They repeated most of the criticisms aired above, and went on to rant about the current nature of organisational life in universities, particularly in relation to research. Despite my attempts to talk specifically about the ERA project, they kept returning to that most familiar of academic complaints: busyness. The journals-ranking system may have been a fiasco, but it merely reflected and was subsumed by the wider problems that academics faced in trying to find time for research in their daily grind. As Sandra, a mild-mannered and obviously disillusioned scholar with over 20 years in the same university, remarked:

> it's impossible to cope with the ever-increasing, ridiculous workloads, and now we have the ERA to contend with. By the time December comes around I'm utterly exhausted but there's still stuff to do like outstanding marking, unit preparation and fixing up the [on-line] blackboard.

Anne, an associate professor, chipped in. 'Yeah. I take a holiday in January, then as soon as I get back it's full on into the teaching stuff. You get loads of emails and inquiries from all and sundry. It drops off around Christmas but then kicks in again soon after.'

Kate, another associate professor in legal studies, added that 'the admin people think we just go off on holiday and swan in for the new semester. If only! There's so much to attend to before the semester even starts.'

I asked Anne about how much research she could do during the break between the end of November and the early February. She glared at me as if I had serious psychiatric disorder, and with just a hint of menace replied:

> Let's put it this way: I co-ordinate a unit with over 700 students with a teaching team of 12, some of whom need a lot of support, others who might drop out, and some who've never taught before. I also teach a masters unit and another small research methods unit. That takes up most of my time ... The emails from students never stop. I get emails at 3:00 or 4:00 in the morning. After preparing for and doing your teaching there's no time for anything else. We also have to oversee casuals that do teaching in the third semester, which used to be our research time.

Sandra and Kate nodded vigorously to these comments, taking occasional gulps of dry white wine. Their glasses were soon empty.

'Another round?', I inquired. This was all beginning to feel depressingly familiar.

As the evening wore on I felt increasingly sorry for these three frazzled tertiary employees. Despite their listless demeanours, they weren't so much depressed as crushed under heavy workloads and excessive managerial scrutiny. Each had entered university bright-eyed and bushy-tailed to make a contribution to knowledge, to try to change a bit of the world. But the cumulative daily demands, frequent disappointments and loss of status had broken their spirits. 'You sort of get on with it, try and get through as best you can and keep your head beneath the parapet and out of trouble. But with things like the ERA there's simply no escape', said Kate, staring into the distance.

'But why not refuse to embrace the bureaucratic demands of the ERA?'

'Not possible', responded Sandra somewhat tersely, as if there was no more to be said. Now that appointments, performance reviews and promotions are increasingly based on various research rankings, it would take a brave soul indeed to take up arms against the might of the ERA, or one's school head or faculty administrator for that matter. So, as in most repressive systems, the repressed subjects embrace the new reality, occasionally attempt to resist it, or simply try to get along as best they can until something better comes along. The problem with this latter course of action is that the status quo can last for a very long time and repressive measures have a way of simply piling up.

Seeking to resist the narrowly quantitative mind-set epitomised by ERA is very hazardous indeed, but playing the 'quality assurance' game only serves to ensure that such systems endure. As I note in chapter 7, there are always alternatives to the current reality, even though regulatory systems are designed to tell you otherwise. The journals-ranking system may have collapsed, but ERA itself – still in its early stages – will continue to radically alter how research and scholarship are conducted in Australian universities, making these activities more restrictive and competitive than ever. This is not a prospect that appeals to many academics.

6

Governing Whackademia

We've been governed in ways that compel us to do the corporate thing and to spend most of our time just trying to keep this place going.

LECTURER IN SOCIAL SCIENCE, QUEENSLAND

We're all administrators now.

SENIOR ACADEMIC IN ARTS, WESTERN AUSTRALIA

Committee work is considered part of 'professional service', but it's just a variation on the theme of administration.

ASSOCIATE PROFESSOR, MELBOURNE

Given the organisational complexities of the contemporary corporate university, the task of keeping the enterprise running is, to say the least, challenging. It involves a variegated army of professional personnel, endless policy statements, procedural rules, and the application of numerous administrative functions, all aimed at cementing the place of universities in the globalised higher education market. In this chapter, I focus on three major aspects of university governance: the application of academic workload formulae (a topic certainly worth revisiting), the role of administration and administrators, and the function of university and particularly school-based committees. Workload formulae are, as I have already noted, key to understanding how academics are governed and how they come to govern themselves, while the other two aspects – administration and committees – illustrate the role played by academics in maintaining universities in their current form. Without these governance mechanisms, it is doubtful whether the modern university could function, but with them academics have to confront the realisation that a considerable amount of their work is devoted simply to keeping their institutions afloat.

The workload vortex

In previous chapters, I briefly discussed the general role of workload formulae in governing the routine aspects of academic life. Here I am more concerned with how these regulatory devices are administered, and the unintended consequences that arise from this process.

Workload formulae made their first major appearance on the university scene in the early 1990s, although some eager institutions had long sought to develop prototype versions of this empirical instrument. The official claim is that workload formulae exist to ensure accountability and transparency. This is strange because, as we shall see, they actually do the very opposite. But administrators and many managers love them. They have become a kind of fetish for the bean-counters who honestly believe that it is possible to quantify work in all its various guises – even though there is not a workload formula in existence that has managed to do so.

One of the main functions of the formulae is to make academic workloads comparable with each other, in order – or so the argument goes – to put an end to exploitative practices, laziness, and corridor bickering. When referring to workload formulae, words like 'equity', 'transparency' and 'fairness' are trotted out by managers who have a stake in ensuring that this empirical device exists, primarily because it allows them to monitor academic staff to the nth degree. Similarly, academic apologists, and especially the para-academics, like work-load formulae because they're a way of keeping an eye on what their colleagues are up to.

Yet it is not too difficult to play the system. Those versed in the art of subterfuge can sometimes exaggerate how busy they are and may insist that they couldn't possibly do anything more because they have been over-loaded over the past three years. Skepticism about the uses to which workload formulae are put was palpable among my interviewees. A senior academic in journalism from a Sydney university let rip on the subjective and divisive nature of workload formulae:

> Ah yes, the workload formula. Utter bullshit of course! Ours are electronic so that anyone in the faculty can see them. The only problem is that the system kept breaking down and failing. No-one could get at the information. [Laughter] Workload formulas are bullshit because like everything else in universities these days, the monitoring of workloads is subject to office politics. Members of the select group get away with

> blue murder while others are constantly held to account. The bureaucrats believe you can deliver measurable outcomes but in terms of fairness and equity, in practice, the workload thing just doesn't work. It's subject to corruption and manipulation. Of course the young academics will do anything to get ahead. And when they get promoted they make sure that they carry out the agenda of the university – which is to make academics jump through the hoops.

According to this academic, workload formulae are integral to top-down mechanisms of governance employed by school heads so that they can maintain order and compliance:

> Heads of school have huge power; they're like little kings and queens. And of course this sort of power is always subject to abuse ... There's no debate about it. It's what the head of school wants and that is that. Often though, you have to second guess what the head of school wants because even he or she might not know. But those in the group seem to know.

Another academic, a youthful aspirant from a school of social sciences in Queensland noted that what upset her the most was that the formulae tended to miss the day-to-day realities of the working day:

> The workload documents are a bit of a joke. The routine stuff that occurs during the course of any one day rarely figures in one's official workload. I would say that at least a quarter of the things we do are not accounted for in the workload document. Many things are not factored into the calculation – like the real amount of time it takes to prepare units for delivery,

> things like photocopying, preparing for teaching sessions. We get allocated the same number of hours for unit preparation irrespective of the number of students we deal with. I don't know how they get away with that one. But this varies across schools. In other schools they do things differently.

The last point raises some interesting questions, given that universities seem to be so pre-occupied with standardising everything, but somehow remain oblivious to the variations in workload calculations that exist across faculties and schools. As a humanities academic from New South Wales commented:

> The funny thing is when it comes to workloads it can be a bit of a free-for-all. In some schools if you finish your PhD you get allocated something like 350 research hours per annum. This is designed to get you to publish. You also get paid at the level B range whereas I am paid at level A and have far less research hours allocated.

Despite the fact that workload formulae were supposedly designed to ensure transparency, mystery persists over precisely what one's colleagues might be doing at any given time. As a somewhat agitated associate professor in a South Australian law faculty told me:

> No-one really knows what anyone else is doing. The workload documents make no sense. The documents are assessed by a workloads committee, and they recommend what changes should be made to the document. The committee takes up a lot of time deliberating upon our workloads and of course being a member of the committee is factored into workloads. Bizarre isn't it!? We only have a small group of staff, so I'm

> not sure why we need this sort of nonsense. They weight your various activities, but most of the time I have no real idea why they have weighted this or that bit of work.

Such problematic practices often lead to bitterness and considerable sniping between colleagues who suspect and often accuse each other openly of favouritism and cronyism. But, as noted, it was the existence of 'ghost work' – the routine, unacknowledged bits of the daily grind – that most irked academics.

Everyone knows that ghost work exists, but it fails to be acknowledged in the formal accounting process. A senior business and commerce academic from regional Victoria noted that a lot of work activities seemed to escape managerial notice:

> things like form-filling, answering emails which can take up to 2 to 3 hours a day – and it's all admin related. If you want to book a room you have to fill in a form, then contact the relevant administrator; if you want to order a laptop or projector there are weighty forms that take time to complete. You might want some IT help: again, you have to access the right place and person, and complete yet another form.

But it's not simply a matter of requesting something. It seems academics now have to negotiate access to any desired service or resource:

> You're not just granted stuff, you have to negotiate things. You might need to register or log on to access the relevant form which is often hidden away in some obscure corner of the university website. All this takes time and means less time to prepare for teaching, and less time for research and other core activities.

Another scholar, a lecturer in chemistry, highlighted the presence of ghosts in his workload machine: 'It's all the stuff associated with teaching. A lot of it simply isn't counted.'

'Like what?', I inquired?

'Ah, let me see, plagiarism management, entry of scores on spreadsheets, ad hoc student inquiries outside consultation times, dealing with appeals and so forth.'

I asked the glaringly obvious question: 'So why do you go along with it? Why not seek to readjust your workload?'

'Well', he replied, 'you can't adjust something that apparently doesn't exist, and to make it exist you'd have to argue your case at the staff committee where the head of school is likely to get irritated or assert that it is covered in another part of the workload calculation.'

This sort of surreal eventuality only makes sense within a system that uses workload calculations even though they are generally regarded as 'imperfect' and incapable of addressing those shadowy or absent bits of information that render it so.

Clearly, this Dali-esque scenario did not sit well with the chemistry boffin, whose blood pressure seemed to be heading rapidly north. As she began talking about 'shifting goalposts' her face went from light pink to cherry red:

> You get to your workload document after much stress and negotiation about two-thirds the way through the preceding semester. It's negotiated with an admin person, then sent to the head of school or whoever for ratification. But what often happens is that two weeks before the new semester the workload is altered because of new circumstances: new student enrolments, financial estimates, whatever. So your 100 per cent workload now becomes 110 or 120 per cent. You work above

> the agreed threshold and there's no time to grapple with this because the teaching is upon you.

This sort of pressure is intensified by the fact that some academics get in first with their workload bids in order to pull what amounts to a fast one over the school head. Thus, the artful dodger might record that over the coming year he or she intends to moderate four of five courses. 'In effect', remarked my anguished interviewee, 'this means they get 50 hours or more of free time because they never do the moderation and it's rarely, if ever, followed up. They know they can get away with it, especially if the head of school is off their back.'

There are other ways of circumventing the workload calculus, and it comes through simply ignoring it and/or devising work methods that loosen its regulatory grip. Given the central importance of workload formulae in one's professional life it probably appears strange of me to admit that I have never read my own 'agreed', 'negotiated' workload documents, not that I can actually remember negotiating anything with anyone. I took what many might consider to be a high-risk approach. Thus, in the event of having been allocated additional work, I simply did less in other areas – obviously without telling anyone. So for example, I might attend a committee once a month rather than twice, or forgo them altogether (until reined in of course). Or I would postpone a grant application until the next round, or not write a planned article. Alternatively, if asked directly about my work – something which occurred on very few occasions – I would exaggerate my contribution or assert that my last workload calculation proved way too burdensome and injurious to my health.

These sorts of simple tactics worked rather well for me. I found that the less information I gave to administrators who presided over the workload calculation, the better. It was all a matter of fighting for the space required to do what I wanted to do, which was teach and research. Broadly, I took the view, as articulated by a lecturer in anatomy in metropolitan New South Wales, that 'Workload formulas have been designed first and foremost to give managers oversight of academics ... The rhetoric of equity and fairness is a ruse. Faced with this, you have to be a strategic or else you'll just get overwhelmed.'

Yet this view was not shared by a small number of the academics I interviewed. One in particular argued that without the workload formulae there would be 'anarchy', and that unscrupulous academics would slink off and neglect their teaching and research duties. When I pointed out that the system could still easily be subverted by clever tacticians and that school heads did not treat everyone equally, he replied, 'Yeah, I get that, it happens all the time, but it's better than nothing'.

Older academics, on the other hand, remembered times before workload formulae existed. Then, as noted in an earlier chapter, more informal regulatory practices operated through a more collegial and unified approach to academic work and through a certain pride in one's profession. Another senior academic, Peter, believed that some form of workload calculation was necessary to achieve 'transparency', so long as it was grounded in a more 'realistic approach': 'Look, I think there are strong grounds for some kind of workload formula. I think some things are measurable, but certainly not everything.' However, even he noted the pitfalls of the system in practice:

> As a result of an Enterprise Bargaining Agreement we are meant to work for 1725 hours per year. This is calculated on the basis of 37.5 hours per week multiplied by 48 weeks plus 4 weeks holiday leave. The problem with the current formula is that managers are telling academics what counts, what sorts of measurement scales should be used – 40 minutes to mark an assignment, 1 hour for student consultation and

> so forth. Managers decide on weightings and time allocation, and administrators enforce this. The problem with this sort of approach is that it fails to take stock of all the things that happen on a daily basis. You need flexibility to take account of the unpredictable things that occur and the normal run of events like chatting, going to the toilet etc. Managers generally have no idea of what we are doing – the amount of time we spend responding to emails, dealing with students and so on. This sort of reductionist way of thinking, reducing things to 15 minute blocks, really is nonsense. This is no way to treat professional people.

And Peter concluded by pointing out some of the wider ramifications:

> As a result of workload formulas and the rest, academics have essentially become outworkers in their own places of work. We fit into a factory model. We're like robots. Administrators now really run the show while we have lost our professional standing, although it is managerial incompetence and our disengagement that has allowed this to happen.

The great contagion: administration and administrators

If academics have indeed stepped away from some aspects of university governance, they have certainly embraced others – most notably, administration. Administration is a necessary part of organisational life. Even admin-phobes like me accept that. But there are limits, and Australian universities have grossly exceeded these over recent years. So much so in fact that administration in all its manifestations has now become an end in itself, and administrators the new organisational supremos of surely one of the most bureaucratised workplaces on planet earth.

Thanks to the adoption of the business model, micro-management and all the other paraphernalia of the 'audit culture', academics now find themselves ensnared in an iron cage from which there appears little prospect of escape. As noted in previous chapters, various monitoring practices have been devised to ensure that an academic's life has been transformed from that of a relatively free-wheeling scholar to a largely office-bound thrall of forms, spreadsheets, histograms and bell curves. To make matters worse, on-line capability has generated more rather than less administrative work for academics, partly because everything is now computerised, and even more form-filling is expected to be done by academics rather than administrative staff.

'We have more administrators than ever', remarked a disgruntled political scientist, 'but all academics do is administration. How can this be? How much administration can a university do?'

Enough, one might answer, to employ an entire army of administrators, to the point where in many institutions their numbers now outstrip those of full-time academics. I asked a peace studies academic of 30 years standing whether he had noticed an increase in administrative duties.

'Well', he responded, 'absolutely, it's been a quantum leap from when I first started at university. The forms have gotten larger and there are far more of them, and now we do everything on-line.'

Without exception, the major complaint emanating from my respondents was the arduous and time-consuming task of accessing and completing forms. They sheeted home the blame for this to the rise of what one academic referred to as 'the endless, obsessive preoccupation with recording and measuring everything'. It wasn't just the quantity of forms that bothered academics, but their complexity and the fact that academics rather than administrators have been increasingly required to complete them.

But how onerous can such demands be? Is all this just hot air? Form-filling can't be that bad, can it?

Thanks to my various contacts at universities across Australia I was able to get some idea of the profound 'form funk' that seems to have enveloped academics. I accessed a range of forms which are usually arranged in alphabetical order on the human resources and finance websites of each university. All you have to do is click on the relevant document and up pops the bureaucratic artifact like a jack-in-the-box. You then find yourself confronted by neat scripts, usually in size 10 or 12 font, Times New Roman or Arial. Boxes of various shapes and sizes pervade the document, instructing you to enter the requested information. In some cases, failure to enter information on-line – and these days most forms are on-line – means that the form comes straight back to you with instructions in red, as happens when you try unsuccessfully to book a flight with a budget airline. Less sophisticated processes can mean that days or weeks go by before the form is sent back to you or, if you're lucky, you'll get a friendly call from a real person somewhere in the bowels of human resources asking you to complete the relevant box.

It's worth pointing out that human resources and finance offices are only two sources of form proliferation. School heads and school administrators have their own private stash. So virulent is the contagion of forms in universities that some academics – or, more expectedly, para-academics – proudly devise their own versions. To demonstrate the sorts of administrative demands we are talking about here, I have assembled a selection of forms, templates and applications from several university sources. These are a distillation of only a tiny fraction of the suffocating miasma billowing out from these institutions:

- Application to drive a university vehicle
- Alcohol on university premises form
- Annual leave in lieu of leave loading application form
- Cash payment for long service leave application
- Employment personal details form
- Employee qualifications form
- Fixed-term appointment nomination form
- Incident, hazard and accident report form
- Induction forms (various and multiple)
- Leave application form
- New staff personal details from outside work application
- Movement request for official travel
- Probation report for academic employees
- Privacy complaint: Internal review application form
- Recommendation for occupancy – adjunct/visiting academics
- Request to advertise
- Request for payout of excess leave
- Qualification form
- Salary sacrificing application
- Special studies leave application
- Talent pool search request form
- Travel insurance claim form
- Training and development needs report form.

And so on and so forth.

Like most forms in other parts of the modern world, many of the above are accompanied by a swathe of guidelines and explanatory notes that make the annual TaxPack look like holiday reading. A sensible person might conclude that, if the form needed this much explanation and qualification, then either the form was poorly constructed or the process requiring it was so complex that a Royal Commission might be more appropriate to assess it. But for the academic seeking study leave there is simply no choice. You have to know what is required because any hint of ignorance or misinformation can spell disaster for the applicant.

In the corridors of Whackademia it is glaringly obvious when academics are completing study leave application forms, because they disappear from the face of the earth for several weeks on end – almost as long as the leave itself – as they try and navigate various notes and guidelines, seek to tick each box, and complete lengthy rationales, justifications and budget statements. Obtaining study leave at most universities these days is about as easy as scaling the north face of Everest. Personal details, evidence of intended outcomes, teaching coverage arrangements, risk assessment, accommodation details and academic contacts all have to be supplied. Once the draft form is completed, it goes to the head of school – who invariably finds fault – and the form is returned to the applicant for yet another go. All this is preceded by what amounts to an exploratory interview with the school head.

During my second (failed) application for study leave, I was initially questioned about my motives by a very assertive administrator and then interrogated by an even more inquisitive school head.

'Why do you think the university should give you time and money for study leave?' was the opening inquiry.

'Well, er, er', I spluttered, 'I want to complete a book on ...'

Before I had time to finish my sentence, the head retorted 'That's not research!'

'Isn't it?', I blathered.

'No', she affirmed with all the authority of a night-club bouncer.

I had thought that accessing secondary sources, deciphering information, engaging in theoretical reflection and participating in intellectual dialogue with one's colleagues constituted a sort of research.

Clearly, I was mistaken. Perhaps it was just airy-fairy scholarship – that at least was what the head's demeanour appeared to suggest.

For most academics the proliferation of forms feels like an interminable demand that can never be sated. As a criminologist from Victoria remarked, 'It's like constantly feeding the form-fiend'. She explains:

> There are endless requests for information in the modern tertiary institution. These include demands to produce a detailed list of your annual publication output (complete with photocopies of every bit of front matter and contents page and affiliation details) and if you are unable to demonstrate all of these essential criteria to prove that you did indeed author each humble published piece then there is a statutory declaration type form to cover such omissions.

These sorts of pressures were compounded by the need to meet rigid deadlines:

> Then there are the forms plus supplementary info for subject outlines, textbook request forms, centrally scheduled exam details – all due each and every semester. There are deadlines to complete the annual staff appraisal document which can run to twenty pages and more attachments, such as your travel plans – annual leave, conference attendance, research field trips – for the next year to be appended …
>
> The problem with this hungry beast is that – to mix the metaphors – the traffic is all one-way. Administrative and management staff send out the demands and the obedient academics oblige, but there is rarely any acknowledgement of all this information – except when one has failed to submit

> the correct form at the appropriate time. For my annual staff appraisal I duly completed several travel request forms and leave forms of varying descriptions to cover the couple of meager occasions when I will be absent from campus for 2011. These *must* accompany the professional development review documents and the boxes were duly ticked at the time of my review. I assumed – perhaps incorrectly – that it is safe to leave the building.

Getting through the thicket of travel administration was perhaps the most galling experience for this academic:

> Now it comes time to book travel arrangements for a field trip on a current research project, and I realise that there is no form granting me permission to leave – the form fiends taketh but never giveth back. Will my position implode as I get on that plane bound for a round of sweaty interviews and data collection in the tropical north? I have just wasted another hour doing a memo, printing out the travel request form and the leave form – none of which have boxes, by the way, to cover *research* leave – gosh a form for academics without such an option – and completing same all over again just in case.

If organising travel is difficult, navigating the administrative demands associated with teaching is excruciating. Ask any academic about how much pressure is involved in presiding over large units, or any units for that matter, and they will use words like 'terrible', 'overwhelming', 'mind-blowing', 'insane' and 'relentless'. Unit assessors who oversee large units involving numerous casual staff are amongst the most stressed-out workers in the tertiary sector. How so? It's not just that they are pressured by teaching and learning personnel and staff in the distance education office to get their unit information guides in on time (times which usually suit the administrative system, rather than the academic), but they also have to keep abreast of enrolments, upload the unit guides and other student-related data onto the departmental webpages, seek out and recruit casual staff, set up on-line student groups and discussion boards, identify topics for weekly discussion and on-line marking columns for tutors, as well as put out spot-fires when they arise – as they inevitably do.

Most spot-fires come in the form of student complaints, fixing omissions and other problems in information guides, finding replacements for sick tutors, and dealing with inevitable breakdowns in internet communication. Remember, all this comes on top of the many overarching routine duties undertaken by academics. It is also worth noting that preparations for a forthcoming semester have to begin well in advance, which means that just as you enter final grades for the one semester, you have to set about preparing for the next. This is why academics talk, as they did in chapter 4, of never-ending teaching. What they're really referring to is never-ending admin.

Another daunting aspect of teaching-related administration is the on-line marking of essays and up-loading of grades for the board of assessors. The processes involved are truly mind-boggling. First, students have to upload their assignments – with the appropriate plagiarism check – which the marker then uploads onto his or her desktop. Each essay is then marked using tracking and eventually uploaded and sent back to the student, and the marker then enters the result on an on-line grade book. Alternatively, the marker can download the assignment, print it out and mark the hard copy, which can then be photocopied on a hi-tech photocopier which automatically turns it into a pdf document, which can then be put on a USB, up-loaded and then sent back to the student. The grand finale of this process is the uploading of final grades for the board of assessors at the end of each semester. All grades are downloaded from the on-line grade book and then placed in a spreadsheet, and then uploaded again for the attention of the board of assessors. Invariably, problems arise during this process, and frequently grades may not appear in front of board members until the last minute – sometimes not at all.

Not that all administrative tasks are as complicated as this, although the general business of administration is multifarious and constant. The latest imposition on academics is the introduction of portfolios that are prepared for the Performance Management Development Review. These take approximately two full weeks to set up and involve a detailed report covering all areas of work. This can then be updated and altered annually in preparation for the review. As one academic commented: 'It's one thing on top of another and the people who devise these sorts of things have no idea how stressful they make our lives. They're more concerned with "streamlining" systems and making life easier for administrators and school heads.'

Power shifts

A number of academics I spoke to said they had given up on certain activities like conference travel or research fieldwork simply because the task of completing forms to undertake such things was too onerous. As one senior academic from Melbourne told me:

> You quickly develop an aversion to form-filling because there are so many of them, so you avoid them as best you can, which means you lose out on a lot of things that you'd like to do – like attend conferences. The conference form at our place runs to 10 pages, most of it justifying why you're going.

But it wasn't simply the emergence of what many considered as an 'over- administered work culture' that concerned most academics as much as the growing power and influence of administrators in the management of day-to-day academic affairs. Academics get especially miffed when administrators comment on substantive matters relating to course/unit design and content, the appointment of casual staff, conference attendance, study leave, media comment, workload and grade distributions. Even those administrators charged with routine tasks like compiling travel claims or processing stationery forms often stray into what were once strictly academic concerns, while more senior staff like school administrators or 'personal assistants' have become close confidants of school heads, occasionally operating in a sort of managerial closed shop. In some schools, the head administrator has close working relations with both course co-ordinators and the school head, often socialising with them outside of work hours and sharing stories about recalcitrant staff. They might even form ad hoc 'management groups' in order to make important decisions affecting the school, particularly when it comes to the all-important budget. In one university I worked at this sort of group acted like a clandestine gaggle of freemasons, making sure that no minutes were taken of their meetings and sharing secret on-line communications rather than ritual handshakes.

Try as they might, it is difficult these days for academics to avoid the undue influence of administrators in their work. They are situated at various points in the management hierarchy, with the most influential in terms of day-to-day management being those clustered around school heads, deans, pro-vice chancellors and vice chancellors. Many administrators are also to be found involved in certain corporate activities such as enrolment, examinations, finance, grants, equal opportunities, risk management, marketing and recruitment, community engagement, and health and safety. That said, administrators are part of a more general culture of administration which involves just about everyone in the tertiary system, including academics. Yet so pre-eminent have administrative supremos become – in terms of their numbers and decision-making powers – that academics (at least those concerned with actually doing academic work) feel like spokes in a giant wheel.

Quite why all this has occurred was a matter of great interest to Barry, a very learned associate professor in business and management in New South Wales. Barry worked for a long stretch as a public servant, then as an industry advocate, and nearly two decades teaching courses on leadership and organisational skills to business and management students. To put it bluntly, he knew what he was talking about. His reflections on university organisational culture, culled from bitter experience, empirical studies and theoretical reflection, offer considerable insight into some of the problems that beset today's universities

Firstly, he explains the rise of administrators to organisational prominence by alluding to the 'shallow pool' of university managers who, because of their apparent inexperience or ineptitude, have enabled a managerial 'gap' to appear. This has been filled by administrators who have usurped managerial decision-making or have a heavy influence upon it. But the real problem, says Barry –and this point has been made by dozens of my respondents – is the disengagement of academics from university governance. Administrators have gained more status than academics in universities over recent years because of a seriously widening power imbalance.

'What', I asked Barry, 'are these powers that have been usurped by administrators?'

> Well, they can adjudicate on workload matters, decide whether casual staff should be employed, and they're in

> cahoots with the school head; they decide whether certain units are viable in light of student numbers and preside over the school budget, the latter often being kept secret from academic staff.
>
> School administrators also keep an eye on applications for various things, even study leave, as well as the more routine stuff like who gets what resources. They work very closely with school heads. They can be scary at times and I often think they have far more say on academic matters than they should.

'Like what?', I asked.

'Like how study guides are structured in terms of length, and which semester units should be taught in. They are also prone to commenting in staff meetings on many routine academic matters.'

Barry was insistent that the role of administrators had exceeded what he thought they should be doing – which was to administer, 'not to have direct power over academics'.

This situation, says Barry, has been compounded by 'the lack of involvement of academics in the whole process of management. They don't want a bar of management and therefore allow policies and practices to slip through that otherwise might have been seriously questioned.'

Barry was particularly scathing about senior academics – 'the professoriate'. It was they, he claimed, who had:

> walked away from key positions in the university. It's not that they're fearful or don't care, they just don't want to engage with management so they drift away from academic governance. It's a tragedy for universities. If you want to turn universities into good workplaces, you have to be engaged ... Increasingly a lot of the key committees here are led by lower-

ranked academics, not professors who have largely opted out of university governance.

Whether or not this is true across the sector is difficult to say, but it seems reasonable to surmise that, given the rise of top-down line management and powerful administrators, this might discourage many academics from participating in key aspects of university governance. Or, if they do, it may be for reasons of promotion rather than commitment to organisational efficiency.

Amid this power shift, there is one group of academics who have few qualms when it comes to doing administration – the para-academics; or, as one Brisbane-based scholar called them, the 'aca-bureaucrats'. The academics who make up this obsequious group, already mentioned in passing throughout this book, have become today's university archetypes. I call them para-academics because they do little or no research, and devote themselves with feverish intensity to form-filling, co-ordination duties and committee attendance. They are characterised by an uncompromising devotion to administrative activities, irrespective of the pain inflicted upon themselves and others by stressful work regimes. For the para-academic, adherence to authority is the name of the game. Like the rest of us, they dislike many aspects of administration, but overall they regard such work as pivotal to the smooth functioning of the university. Without complex systems of administration – form-filling, monitoring and endless evaluation – the system would surely implode, would it not? Not surprisingly, their closest relationships are with other administrators and the school head.

Para-academics are particularly partial to staff meetings, as it is there that they can display the full range of their administrative talents. The staff meeting is in fact only one of a number of meetings attended by para-academics and others who deal with routine aspects of university governance. These include meetings both in and out of the school context, like the ethics committee, promotions committee, academic board, programs committee, school board, board of assessors, the teaching and learning committee, grants committee, management group, and so on. But the staff meeting is one of the main hubs for school-based administrative decisions outside less structured forums like co-ordinators' meetings and private liaisons between para-academics and school heads.

Staff meetings are events like no other on the university calendar. Held monthly, academics, administrators, heads of school, specially invited guests (often the faculty dean or teaching and learning experts), and sometimes student representatives come together for two hours or more to deliberate on all matters relating to the school. Most staff meetings possess an air of deep foreboding, mainly because budgetary matters typically tend to dominate proceedings. Once the head of school begins to outline the latest fiscal tragedy, everyone leans forward to await the ensuing edict. It's as if their professional lives depended on such matters – which in many ways, they do. Para-academics love this sense of impending doom, it's why they get up in the morning. They seek out dramas because they can then rally to the assistance of the school head by doing the necessary ameliorative work – usually a lengthy response to a curly inquiry or a string of recommendations in a glossy report. But despite their love of staff meetings, even para-academics can at times find them terminally boring. Because of their inherent tedium, staff meetings invite acts of disrespect: feigned yawns, sniggers, rib-digging, doodling, rolling of eyeballs, note-passing, head-scratching, nose-picking and occasional snoring.

The meetings are usually chaired by the school head, and on other occasions by para-academics themselves. The actual process involves going through the agenda via apologies, confirmation of the minutes of the previous meeting, and discussion of items, many of which have been encountered on numerous previous occasions. As meetings proceed, people come and go for a variety of reasons: some feign urgent business elsewhere and usually clatter into the door on their way out, much to the annoyance of the school head; others require a toilet break or need to send an urgent SMS. The chairperson plays a key role in proceedings by monitoring contributions and occasionally putting an end to discussions, sometimes just as they are about to get interesting. Para-academics and those with vested interests – which is just about everyone – are drawn in and out of points of discussion. Some of the more ambitious academics try to intercede to make sure their faces are recognised and voices heard, since a positive attitude toward staff meetings always impresses the school head, and the para-academic.

Less committed members may surreptitiously take out essays and start marking them, peering up every now and again to convey the impression that they are involved in proceedings. Throughout, there is constant clock-watching, especially as the meeting enters its second hour. Yawns and head scratching increase, as does shuffling in seats. As meetings trudge on, a discursive pattern arises that is obvious to all: namely, that only a few do most of the talking. Occasionally, an attempt is made to exercise democratic process through a vote. This takes everyone by surprise and always falls into chaos because voting protocols are rarely talked about, meaning that when it comes to putting forward a motion no-one really knows how to. But it is too easy to be cynical about such things. While frequently farcical, staff meetings do play an important role in school governance, if only to confirm the main players and the potholes that need to be avoided.

Staff meetings' darkest moments come when issues of income generation and the school budget are raised. Any downturn in student enrolments or immanent budgetary crisis is greeted with sombre reflection and urgent calls for action. But even at the best of times, the underlying concern is with balancing the books. For instance, teaching issues invariably dovetail with financial concerns. That is why staff meetings – like teaching and learning committees, school boards and examiners' committees – spend so much time developing strategies to lower attrition rates through ever-more creative means of persuasion, learning support and flexible delivery. The simple logic goes something like this: departing students equals financial shrinkage, which means tighter budgets and less resources for things like conference attendance and study leave. In short, academics have a direct personal interest in keeping students on the books.

Similarly, as discussed in chapter 4, the pursuit of quality assurance in relation to teaching fulfils much the same purpose: it seeks to ensure that students are as supported as they can be through a remarkable array of remedial services. If they continue with their studies, they contribute to Equivalent Full-Time Student calculations. To be sure, students might 'learn' a lot from such support – stuff like basic literacy and communication skills, which by rights they should have been exposed to well before entering university – but the dominant rationale is retention, come what may.

But I digress, the salient point about staff meetings is that they are amateurish, slightly theatrical affairs that sometimes manage to make some meaningful decisions – but mostly not. It is a commonly held view among academics that these ritualised gatherings could be conducted less often and in shorter time-frames without any appreciable difference to the functioning of any given school.

The fact that money matters so preoccupy staff meetings is hardly surprising. There was not a meeting I attended in the past ten years where some sort of immanent fiscal tragedy wasn't revealed or calls for belt-tightening made. Recently – and especially since the worrying decline in full-fee-paying overseas students – expenditure on anything but the most essential of academic activities has been curtailed. Perhaps not surprisingly, application forms for conference attendance and study leave have increased in size over the years as budget constraints have kicked in. At many universities, academic leave applications are viewed by managers and administrators with great suspicion. So much so in fact that at the top of the policy statement regarding special studies leave at Southern Cross University is the statement that such leave is 'granted as a privilege and not as a right' – as if anyone needed to be reminded of this patronising edict.

Even those meetings that purport to be about serious scholarly matters – faculty meetings, academic board, programmes committee, school board – are weighed down with financial concerns about whether this or that programme or unit is 'marketable' or how many student enrolments make a unit 'viable'. Perhaps the most depressing staff meeting I attended during the course of my 25-year career was at SCU when a history unit in the school of arts and social sciences, which was experiencing low student enrolments, was unceremoniously axed, without as much as a whimper from academics who sat around the table. Actually that's not quite true. A young casual staff member attempted to point out some home truths to the assembled throng:

> Why are we dropping these units when under this [Howard] government history is under the greatest assault? Shouldn't we be defending these units? We surely need history units in the arts and social science programme, don't we? I really don't understand what is happening here.

There was some shaking of heads, but certainly no impassioned responses to this belated defence of what in other eras would have been regarded as an indispensible offering. Instead, an awkward, resigned silence prevailed, eventually giving way to the next agenda item. I also sat there and said nothing because, like others, I felt utterly deflated by a short-sighted decision based solely on market-driven considerations. In a system that values units for their own sake, rather than their market utility, it is inconceivable that such a destructive act could have occurred. Yet, as one emeritus professor in the natural sciences from a Queensland university remarked:

> A monetary value is attached to everything these days. If a unit has got low numbers, out it goes, irrespective of whether it possesses content which academics consider educationally important and therefore worth retaining. We used to teach small units and no-one batted an eyelid, but now all that has changed.

It certainly has. Over recent years, many worthwhile units and programs in peace and conflict studies, social ecology, women's studies, history, classics and languages have bitten the dust. Instead, we have witnessed the emergence of a new generation of demand-led courses in the United States, Britain and Australia: Arguing with Judge Judy; Alien Sex; David Beckham Studies; FemSex; UFOs in American Society; Philosophy and Star Trek; Cyberporn Society; Ghost Busting; Learning from YouTube; Golf Management; Lego Robotics; Queer Musicology; Digital Games; Sports Ministry; Surfing Studies; The Simpsons and Philosophy; Whitewater Skills; Reflexology; Aromatherapy; Oprah Winfrey: The Tycoon; American Pro Wrestling; Campus Culture and Drinking; Spiritual Healing; Traditional Chinese Herbal Medicine; and – my personal favourite – The Phallus.

But even in the context of narrow rationalities, it is worth asking what constitutes an acceptable and cost-effective number of students in a unit? As I discovered – by dint of my participation in numerous meetings! – the cut-off figures vary from one institution to another, as well as within universities themselves. A lecturer from a university in Melbourne told me that:

> there is absolutely no standardised practice for anything at all [here], each program has different targets and each of these targets will be assessed with varying degrees of flexibility, depending on who is looking at it. Part of the problem is that the goalposts are never clear or stable.

Another academic, this time a retiring social science professor in South Australia, admitted 'I have no idea what the cut-off figure is, 10 perhaps ... There's no set figure.' And a senior lecturer in commerce in New South Wales noted 'there are numerous criteria around the uni but a general rule of thumb is 15 students'. In short, there are no universal cut-off criteria. Rather, the decision to axe units turns on an amorphous range of market-driven considerations. This means, in effect, that it is entirely unclear, even in a system so obsessed with measurement and standardisation, which units might survive or not, and on what basis. Clearly, one year's slump may not signal the death of any given unit, but two or three years of low enrolment numbers may lead to the chop. It is then that units are guillotined on the basis that they are 'unviable', 'untenable' or – horrors of horrors – not 'cost effective'.

Such considerations go some way to explaining those awkward moments in staff meetings when the grisly matter of school budget is raised. Typically, unit co-ordinators of suspect units begin to tremble as the grave school head or administrative supremo issues the latest announcement of a fiscal crisis. Furtive glances are exchanged and there is much shifting in seats. The most pronounced bodily sensations are experienced by nervous co-ordinators – eyes averted, shoulders slumped, stomaches churning – as they steel themselves for the impending interrogation of their unit's low enrolment members.

It is at such times that managers and administrators tend to join forces in a kind of micro-organisational pincer movement that forces the reluctant academic to explain why their offerings have such low public appeal and what they intend to do in order to sex things up. The last time I witnessed such a display was when a feisty co-ordinator of an introductory sociology unit with surprisingly low numbers went into full counter-attack, accusing all and sundry of failing to understand the enormous importance of her unit as foundational to the world as we know it. Even the tough-as-nails head of school buckled at this point, promising to discuss the matter in private. Suffice to say, there was no more open talk about the unit's pathetic numbers, and we were all left with the vague hope that next year's intake would finally justify its existence. As far as I know the unit's enrolment numbers still hover somewhere near to a mysterious cut-off point, although the matter is now subject to in-house sub judice, and will remain so for some time to come.

The point about such encounters is that they often reveal the underlying nature of relations between academic staff and their managers and administrators, especially when the latter appear to be in cahoots on academic matters. Tensions can often arise in such situations. A number of my respondents noted that relations with some senior administrative staff are sometimes severely strained. Roger, an associate professor in environmental studies with abundant experience of various universities, noted:

> Administrators have very little regard for academics. I'd say that 90 per cent of them can't stand academics. They think we

> have it easy, going off to conferences and the like. They think that all we do is teach. They don't understand the rest of the things we do like research and writing.

The majority of academics I spoke to referred to the occasional 'helpful', 'nice' and 'supportive' administrators, who went out of their way to assist with things like photocopying, stationery allocation and on-line grade entries. But the general perception was of on-going tensions between academics and administrators, brought on by the diminished status of the former in relation to the latter and the omnipresence of stifling bureaucratic demands. Many academics felt disempowered by the growing power of administrators, particularly when it comes to the imposition of on-line bureaucracy. As one civil engineering scholar told me:

> I'm 57, and have taught for 20 years. The thing that is really pissing me off most is the constant administrative techno-systemic creep that sets the conditions in which co-ordinators operate. We have all the responsibility but are increasingly told what to do by administrative services that have none. There is no-one to complain to and no redress.

Needless to say, such tensions are certainly not assisted by Machiavellian heads of school, whose character assassinations of some academics can negatively alter the perceptions of administrators, thereby ensuring that the targeted scholar gets short shrift when it comes to administrative affairs. Thus administrators responsible for room bookings, the stationery cupboard, and contracts and leave applications may slow up the processing of staff requests or ignore them altogether. As Stan, a somewhat bitter senior lecturer in engineering, remarked:

> These days you have to be very careful about what and how you say things to administrators. If you put one of them offside, the rest can follow. If one of them dislikes you, you might be allocated the most remote lecture theatre on campus or find yourself teaching late on a Friday afternoon.

Perhaps the last word about the fraught nature of academic–administrator relations should go to Terry, a highly experienced senior law academic in Brisbane. She reflected:

> The ratio of administrators to academics at my university is about 80:20. They now run the place. Academics are therefore overloaded with surveys, questionnaires and various other tasks ... When I first started [over 20 years ago] you could get heaps of administrative support, but no longer. You have to do it all yourself. Everything is on the computer. There's no more delegation of routine administrative tasks, these are done largely by academics.

Staring into space, Terry concluded: 'Not so long ago I felt as if academics ran the show, but now I think we're just administrative clones but with reduced status. Administrators now run the show.'

Tail wagging the dog indeed!

7

Enough complaint, now what?

We [academics] can't wait for the day when there's some great policy U-turn. We have to carve out space for ourselves and this means changing what we do on a daily basis.

SENIOR LECTURER IN SOCIAL SCIENCE, QUEENSLAND

We have to engage in creative resistance at ground level as well as fight for a different university in the public arena.

SESSIONAL WORKER IN BUSINESS AND TOURISM, NEW SOUTH WALES

It doesn't matter which university or what level of academic you care to consult, complaint is rife throughout Whackademia. But complaint comes from others too: from students, professional associations, members of the general public and, as we shall see, representatives of Australia's business community. They're not complaints simply about under-resourcing of tertiary institutions or the narrow approach to teaching, or even about value for money (a common complaint among overseas students). Rather, the most pressing complaints are to do with the fact that universities tend to churn out graduates who are entirely unprepared either for the world of work – one of the current system's main priorities – or for active participation in everyday civic life.

Partly as a result of such concerns, new institutions of higher education – self-consciously uncoupled from simple economic imperatives – have emerged in Britain and the United States over recent years. These offer an interesting window to how 'higher education' might be alternatively conceptualised and made more relevant in a modern, transformative and globally connected world. In the interim, however, academics in Australia react in various ways to the exigencies of the existing system, some coping and getting by, others resisting or seeking to retire, move on or simply leave.

This chapter outlines these different responses and their consequences, and discusses what happens when complaints are not heeded or simply become too much for the complainant. It also offers some suggestions to those academics who continue to work in Whackademia about how they can seek to offer what might be termed 'creative resistance' that opens up new and more engaging spaces for themselves and others.

Faulty products

Given the ascendancy of the business model in the management of universities, and its links to the economy and allied systems of production, one area that you would expect the tertiary sector to get absolutely right is its engagement with business. After all, universities claim to be the backbone of a modern globalised economy by producing a highly educated and capable workforce.

But, despite industry-relevant curricula, vocationally orientated teaching, 'graduate attributes', swanky student portfolios and the rest, many business leaders think that universities are producing one-dimensional graduates incapable of good communication, teamwork, and independent and creative thought. This view is shared by many commentators on the sector, who point out that the majority of business schools fall well below 'world class' standards as a result of poor teaching and an over-emphasis on vocational outcomes. As one observer noted in *The Age*: 'there are too many slack business schools and lazy academics who refuse to change, barely publish significant research, and lack customer focus'.

A more measured criticism of what goes on in business and other schools has been aired by Michael Andrew, head of a higher education taskforce of the Business Council of Australia. Seeking to muscle in on higher education, Andrew asserts that 'suede patch tenured academics' are more concerned with protecting their domain than helping to produce the highly skilled and knowledgeable graduates required by business, adding that 'we need to work with government and universities to invest in a modern partnership'. Andrew further notes that 'the greater emphasis [by government and universities] on quantity and domestic participation is good ... but we don't want quantity at the cost of quality'. Andrew goes on to employ telling productivist language in his pitch for increased consultation between business and universities: 'I keep saying to universities that I am your major customer. I take 750 of your product each year. I want engagement around what you are teaching ... You need to look at this as a package in the same way as a customer–supplier relationship.'

Also head of one of Australia's largest accounting firms, Andrew is not one to mince his words. Nor is one of his taskforce associates, Paul Douglas, head of a major engineering firm. Approving of the university sector's 'technical' approach to teaching, Douglas argues that a bolder approach to education in general is required: 'It's more about broadening out the curricula to produce people who can work on a range of issues, solve problems and work in teams'. Yet another industry colleague on the taskforce, Michael Quinn, head of a large property group, chucked in his two bob's worth. Students, he claimed, 'are taught not to broaden skills and knowledge but taught to define it'.

With one eye on the 2012 round of deregulation in the sector, and the other on the apparent dangers of over-expansion, Andrew observed that universities appeared self-absorbed and resistant to change – a bit like recidivist juvenile offenders. To break this apparent recalcitrance, Andrew called for a 'modern partnership' between business and the university sector.

Worry as you well might about a corporate accountant, property tycoon and engineer seeking to shape the future of university education in this country, it must be galling for our vice chancellors to be publicly lectured like this by the very people they seem so eager to serve. Yet university chiefs have for some time been aware that industry is not overly impressed with modern graduate 'competencies'. In a 2011 paper titled 'Employer satisfaction of university graduates: Key capabilities in early career graduates', education researchers Mahsood Shah and Chenicheri Nair observe a chasm between the skills and knowledge levels of graduates from one leading metropolitan university and the expectations of the over 700 employers who had taken them on. The authors conclude that there exists:

> a gap between what employers see as most important in terms of the skills, knowledge and attributes of recent graduates and their satisfaction. Some of the key areas identified in the survey where such gaps exist include communication, the organisation of work and managing time effectively, the willingness to face and learn from errors and listening openly to feedback, the ability to set and justify priorities, being flexible and their adaptability and willingness to listen to different points of view before coming to a decision.

Shah and Nair cite a number of studies going back to the early 1990s that similarly highlighted glaring deficiencies in early career graduates.

Time and again, business and education organisations – like the Australian Chamber of Commerce and Industry, the Australian Industry Group, the Department of Education Science and Training, and Graduate Careers Australia – have stressed the need for greater synchronisation between university education and industry, but to no avail. While Universities Australia and Graduate Careers Australia continue to boast about stratospheric undergraduate satisfaction levels, there remains a serious disjuncture between the quality of many of our graduates and the requirements of industry. This is not to say that I support such a cozy alliance between higher education and industry, but if the university sector is so concerned with getting into bed with industry, how has it got the foreplay so terribly wrong? That said, there is little doubt that, with the intervention of the Bradley review, the rise of various quality assurance regimes, and vice chancellors' continued kow-towing to the demands of industry, the tertiary education sector will be brought into line – Australia's economic future depends upon it, or so we're told.

Where to from here?

A lot of academics dislike this association with industry. It makes them feel as if they are part of a wider system of capitalist production – which of course they are. 'What's it all for?', asked one of my alienated colleagues from South Australia. 'We've been dragooned into the production and reproduction of a system which most of us abhor. We make money to keep universities afloat and produce students to meet the demands of the economy.' But the criticisms of universities as product assembly lines are far from new. All the rhetoric about neo-liberal governance, instrumentalism, corporatisation, the enterprise university and so on seems to echo complaints that were being made when I was a student back in the 1970s. Still, things have changed – a lot. The perfect storm of business models, managerialism and edu-metrics which first struck in the early to mid-1980s has created a system characterised by the dualism of glowing official rhetoric on the one hand and a subterranean culture of academic complaint on the other.

The pivotal question here is: where do we go with all this critique, this litany of ugly complaints? We can't really call for a return to a glorious past, since the 'old school' is widely viewed as elitist, patriarchal and middle-class. Anyway, lots of academics back then were complaining about 'the system' or 'the establishment' – views not unlike those of many interviewed for this book. But rather than talk openly about capitalist domination, most academic critics nowadays tend to rage against neo-liberalism and the corporatisation of universities, often ignoring their own role in sustaining such institutions. In many ways, the visions of a different sort of higher education system are as fuzzy today as they were in the Age of Aquarius.

At least most of today's vice chancellors can claim a coherent vision for the future based on a system of high-quality, mass education; a 'republic of learning' that has apparently erased the patriarchal elitism of previous times. Highly questionable as such claims might be, it is clear that the promoters of today's higher education system – policy-makers, senior university managers and administrators – run the show. They have created a mirage of universities that has led some sections of the public into believing such institutions are high-quality intellectual hot-houses. This has been achieved through a steady stream of carefully constructed propaganda and the silencing of academic concerns by confining employee discontent to occasional procedural and industrial disputes or, more commonly, bouts of fruitless private complaint.

Many academics continue to struggle bravely against the worst aspects of Whackademia through their unions (although only about 40 per cent of full-time academics actually belong to the NTEU) but it often feels like the odds are too heavily stacked against them. As I noted in the Introduction, complaints are important ways of informing and achieving change, but if such articulations are too wild and woolly they can be easily disparaged by the powerful. By the same token, the retreat into disengagement hardly helps the cause of change, although some might conceive of this as resistance. In the remainder of this chapter I examine a range of responses among academics to the current realties that face them: survivalism, disengagement and conformity; resistance; over-the-wallism; and paradigm-busting. Each has their own strengths and failings. I then set out where I think there lies the most hope of freeing universities from the current culture of instrumental servitude, and of restoring the soul and sense of active citizenship to higher education. The possibility of a different sort of education, based on passion, interest, public virtue and civic purpose, depends not simply on criticism – however cathartic that might be – but also a vision that persuades, excites, informs and lays the foundations for action and democratic engagement.

Survivalism, disengagement and conformity

As noted throughout this book, ducking beneath the radar of and disengaging from repressive university governance are common forms of behaviour among Australian academics. Some academics choose to survive because they need jobs to pay off debts and to give their life meaning and purpose. For others, it's more a matter of psychological survival. Without at least the appearance of conformity to the prevailing order – meeting performance targets and workload expectations – life as an academic can become rather unbearable. My own experience at Southern Cross University, although painful, was hardly exceptional in today's tertiary sector. Within days of arriving at the Coffs Harbor campus I was advised by a senior administrator not to 'rock the boat' or appear 'subversive'. I learned also about the power that faculty managers possessed and how easy it was to become the subject of their disciplinary attention.

The problem with not being noticed, doing the right thing and generally conforming to expectations is that you lose your soul and, in the process, simply grant more power to your oppressors. Here is an associate professor in education reflecting on survival through 'embodiment':

> There's a kind of hegemony-by-consent in this place. We survive because we have internalised aspects of the regime. Our embodied practices include answering emails at three in

the morning, working at weekends, conforming to workload calculations, and putting in grant applications. University management really doesn't have to do much, we keep the system going – we are the system, even those of us who criticise universities but carry on regardless. We are part of that system. We make the system work.

Precisely why such internalisation of the system has occurred is a story in itself. 'I think that the change originated some time ago', said Rose, a critical theorist and staunch opponent of today's higher education system:

> Neo-liberals were able to change the narrative. The dominant story now falls within the imperatives of globalisation and the economy. Instead of talking about equality, rights, citizenship, and now climate change, we have been co-opted into another story that is about getting students work-ready so that they can take their part in the competitive system of production and consumption. That is our current sphere of operations in the university system ... Without even knowing it, the new hegemony has been created through the language and our embodiment of instrumental practices.

Rose talked further about how the 'critical perspectives that once dominated discussions about educational practice' have been, if not replaced, 'then increasingly overshadowed by a new narrative about work-readiness, career enhancement and the needs of industry'. She pointed especially to the systems of hierarchical management that had ensured conformity to the new order. For Rose, while the adoption of certain practices had enabled most academics to stay the course, it also meant the system could continue to function unimpeded. So while it was possible to consciously disengage from some aspects of the system, this did not mean it was possible to step outside its sphere of influence. It turns out that seeking to survive a system of busyness and corporate management is more about unintended collaboration than survival.

Resistance

Resistance comes in many forms. Its function is to destabilise the existing order by engaging in various acts of dissidence and subversion. Resistance offers the time and space to do what you really want to do, and to constructively subvert managers and apparatchiks in the process. Resistance can be of the in-your-face variety (which is risky) or far more subtle. Either way, it's a hazardous enterprise and so the most carefully considered strategies should be adopted if you are to avoid unwanted managerial attention. As noted in Chapter 2, universities do not like academics who question the 'brand' and its allied processes – that's why they have such elaborate systems of regulation and control in place.

Below I highlight some examples of resistance. Many of these have been drawn from years of personal experience and from what I have heard from countless other academics, including many of the malcontents interviewed for this book. Clearly, I intend some of the following to be merely humourous, and others mischievous; yet others are deadly serious. Whatever approach you adopt, you should do so in the belief that your actions will improve your own institutional experience as well as those of your colleagues and students.

The first set of suggestions relates to ways of subverting the mania for workload measurement:

- Always problematise the workload formula and make this a constant item on the staff meeting agenda.
- Keep adding to and subtracting from your workload documents as, over time, this will exhaust the apparatchiks.
- Join the 'slow' movement.
- Play the academic bureaucrats at their own game by pretending to be doing lots of administration.
- Appear busy by ruffling your hair, walking speedily through corridors and gasping for breath.
- Complain endlessly about how busy you are, as this will deflect attention from the apparatchiks.
- Start an Academic Survivors of Workload Formulae support-group and ask for assistance from university counsellors.
- Claim depression, stress, anxiety disorders, backaches, drug and alcohol problems resulting from excessive workloads.

When it comes to the slavish task of marking, the following paint-balls can be joyously fired:

- Never set assignments over 2000 words (make that 1500), and justify this by spurious arguments about brevity and getting to the point.
- If you want to ensure that all your students get through, provide grid-like instructions which, rather like painting by numbers, smoothes the way for a passable essay.
- Try and restore balance to the current madness by shifting the focus from at-risk to high-achieving students.
- Always question the sacred bell curve and embarrass the rationalists by talking about the social construction of grade distributions; and

- For all full fee-paying students, ask if they would like to receive a mark or a receipt once you have marked their essays.

At staff meetings, while it may be tempting to simply buy an inflatable doll, dress it in your clothes and leave it in your usual seat, this is a tactic only for the very bold. Alternatively, much enjoyment can result from employing the following:

- Disrupt meetings by contesting received ideas. The apparatchiks hate this as it interferes with process.
- Home in on one item and make an obscure point that will impress all, then go back to sleep.
- Never challenge the chair, as he or she will surely target you.
- If you are on a video link, make sure you turn on the mute button, that way you can spend an hour or more lampooning others without them having a clue.
- If there is an item that has serious implications for you and others, scrutinise the details, otherwise see above points.

On the matter of performance reviews, you can gain enormous satisfaction by indulging in the following antics:

- Dispute the very idea of performance reviews and keep highlighting their shortcomings at staff meetings.
- Agitate for peer-based reviews, the use of external moderators, or even self-assessment.
- Always inflate your performance by using words such as 'excellent', 'excellence', 'outstanding', 'major contribution to ...' and so forth.
- Never admit to screw-ups, cock-ups, student complaints, or disagreements with colleagues or managers.

- Always appear totally devoted to the university's goals.
- Exaggerate your commitment: claim, for instance, that your main goal for the next year is to work yourself to a standstill.
- Always assert that you are overworked but are doing your very best in difficult circumstances.
- Always have your union representative in the wings.
- Always thank your faculty manager for this wonderful opportunity.
- Pretend you welcome frankness and honesty.
- Never sign off on critical reports.
- Use all your deconstructivist powers to undermine negative claims; and
- If your manager is a performance review sceptic, you're in business.

Yes indeed, resistance can be jolly good fun and you never know, the irreverence contained in subtle acts of subversion and ridicule might become wonderfully contagious among your more obsequious colleagues.

Over-the-wallism

The over-the-wallers are the university sector's escapees. They are those who are first in line for voluntary redundancies, or those who resign because they quite simply can't carry on because of sheer exhaustion, boredom or existential despair. It is difficult to know how many escapees there are out there, although given the aging of the academic workforce it is no doubt quite a number. The most vocal of escapees are those who object to the current university regime. Their complaints are not too different from those shared by other academics recorded in this book.

My own favorite escapee account – culled from Britain's *Spectator* magazine – comes from Professor Peter Jones, an internationally acclaimed biologist at the University of Cambridge who decided to quit in 1997. Although English, his story could just as easily be that of countless academics in the current Australian university system, hence the inclusion of his account here. Professor Jones began his explanation of why he fled Whackademia with the terse adieu: 'Bugger the system, I'm off'. The reasons for this were complex but basically boiled down to his objection to the oppressive nature of university governance. After savaging the sector's adoption of the business model, Professor Jones highlighted one of its ugly spin-offs:

> since we were now to be regarded as businesses, our 'practices' and 'output' had to be checked, monitored, controlled, evaluated and subjected to 'market forces'. Enter the inquisition. Exit, slowly, loyalty. Further, since it was now the government that was determining our procedures, power in universities began to shift away from the people doing the teaching and researching to the administrators, who were charged with putting more and more government diktats into effect.

This familiar line of complaint is followed by a full-blooded assault on administration supremos whose obsequious role in maintaining systems of regulation added nothing to university life. He lampoons their 'inane vocabulary of business speak, their fantasy worlds built on their fantasy language, the object of derision among both academics and the more intelligent businessmen'. These supremos, says the irate professor, have further helped administer models of institutional integration that enable universities across Britain and Europe to merge their courses, thereby making it possible for easy student transfer in a borderless marketplace. To smooth this process, semesters replaced terms, years became stages, and courses became modules.

But Professor Jones reserved his most scathing comments for the claims made by vice chancellors about pedagogical excellence. He noted the widespread efforts to retain students at any cost and the narrowly constituted curricula that were (and are) offered under the banner of 'higher education'. (Sounds familiar?) All this, according to Professor Jones, 'borders on farce'. Responding to government claims that universities are producing high-calibre graduates, Professor Jones counters, 'No, simply a workforce that has been through the modern university system. It takes a seriously intelligent student to squeeze an education out of it.'

After more critical reflections on the demise of meaningful higher education, Professor Jones comments: 'I am too old for this anti-educational, anti-intellectual nonsense'. Instead, he looked forward to reinventing the past in his post-university life: 'I can hardly wait to get back to those days when going to work did not bring another avalanche of illiterate drivel from quality controllers, bossy demands from administrators to describe the business skills inherent in teaching'.

Armed with a healthy superannuation package, Professor Jones went on to carve out a peaceful and productive life beyond the corporatised tertiary precincts. But 1997 is very different to the advanced systems of oppression witnessed by academics in the tertiary system circa 2012, when the reins of managerial control have been further tightened and universities are ever more determined to protect their patch.

Paradigm-busters

Instead of going over the campus wall, the paradigm-busters want to break it down. They actively seek to overthrow the current system of university education and replace it with something else. These revolutionaries see little hope in attempting to reform what they consider a dastardly market-based system, and they scold those colleagues who acquiesce to it. The irony, of course, is that these same critics often embody aspects of the very system they deride, although if confronted by this awkward fact they will leap instantly to their own defense. Many paradigm-busters are able to articulate a semi-coherent vision of an alternative approach to university education, but others struggle to do so. Above all, they want to break the chains of neo-liberal governance and instead create a new system according to principles drawn from various intellectual utopias ranging from ancient Greece, to the 1960s and more contemporary examples.

Paradigm-busters seek to evoke the idea of university education as a passionate commitment to and interest in ideas that connect to everyday life in a thriving, equitable and just democratic society. They seek to do away with the commodification of higher education, and therefore to detach it from simple economic imperatives. Accordingly, passion, interest, delight, curiosity, dialogue, critique and genuine community engagement replace the current emphasis on money-making, industrial relevance and job readiness. They envision a time when universities would be fully funded by government, campuses central to community life, and courses based on their value to the common good rather than the school budget.

Current revolutionary critiques of tertiary education are many and varied, but are united around a deep yearning for something different. Such hopeful advocates appear like aggrieved aspirants no longer prepared to hang around in purgatory. For them, the waiting game is over. We see signs of such discontent in websites like Unileaks in Australia and Edufactory in the United States. We also see it in the critiques regularly aired in the pages of the *The Australian*'s 'Higher Education' section, *Campus Review, Arena Journal, New Matilda, Australian Universities Review* and *The Advocate.* We even see it embedded in blogs, Facebook and Twitter exchanges, in seminars and conferences, and in autobiographies by the likes of Stephen Fry and Mungo MacCallum – who have highlighted the exuberance of pre-corporate university life in England and Australia respectively.

But today's paradigm-busters are interested in the future more than the past. As such, they attempt to create forums and processes (rather than formal institutions) that celebrate and promote debate around ideas and issues of the day. They are concerned with social justice, human rights and participatory democracy – not the bottom line. They want to do away with rote teaching, and the intrusive monitoring and subsequent zombification of academics. They want a return to community, collegiality, fun, soul and passion. Although not wedded to any specific ideological agenda, paradigm-busters nonetheless are concerned with matters outside the remit of the GDP, economic growth and corporate profit. Let's take a peek at a few examples of paradigm-busters: the Free/Slow University of Warsaw, the Free University of Melbourne, and some progressive colleges in the United States.

The Free/Slow University of Warsaw is one of the many alternatives to the corporatised system of higher education that has swept over Europe in recent years. Describing itself as a 'nomadic', nonprofit institution, the FSUW promotes interdisciplinary studies on social and artistic issues, and invites students to participate in a progressive form of education that is uncoupled from the pursuit of career and profits. It opposes the calculated rapidity and for-profit impulses of globalisation and instead promotes 'freedom through slowness'. Through the wonders of 'bar camps' and 'un-conferences' – which democratise the education process by doing away with the dominance of 'experts' and instead creating ideas trading at market stalls – the FSUW has created a less rigid and more inclusive educational experience, the primary outcomes of which are the joys of learning through critical engagement.

But you don't need to go all the way to Warsaw to experience this sort of forum. The Melbourne Free University was founded in 2010 by some disgruntled academics and postgraduate students. The MFU asserts on its website, that it:

> stands for radical equality: the a priori belief in universal equality and possibilities of emancipation. The Free University is free and accessible. It remains politically and economically autonomous from political parties and organisations, government, private bodies, universities and NGOs.

The folk at the MFU believe that 'people have the responsibility to seek and engage with knowledge. Learning is an act of will and empowerment.'

The very existence of the MFU is based on opposition to the neoliberal agendas of mainstream universities: 'The Free University is an alternative to the exclusive and outcome orientated education sector, enabling the pursuit of knowledge for its own sake, and thereby freedom'. The MFU holds courses on a range of contemporary issues. Its 2011 program on war and peace includes sessions on wars and ending them, fragile states, torture, on killing, peace and non-violent change. The MFU also runs seminars on philosophy, sociology and the cinema, sustainability, Australian identities and – you've guessed it – higher education.

The MFU embraces open, frank and non-hierarchical discussions as a way of learning rather than 'talking head' lectures delivered by experts. MFU's approach to pedagogy seeks 'to offer space for independent engagement with important contemporary ideas and issues'. In contrast to the productivist logic of today's corporate university, the 'outcome' of education for the MFU is the actual process of critical engagement, and the attempt to promote change through knowledge sharing and social action. That said, what is taught at MFU is not necessarily all that different from the content conveyed in some other university courses, but it does differ fundamentally in terms of its underlying pedagogical values. Issues are discussed for their intrinsic interest and with a keen eye on the interconnections between knowledge, action and social change. Knowledge is therefore not wedded to simple instrumental values (career, credentialism, economic growth) or regarded as something to be sold on the open market. It possesses an intrinsic value that celebrates learning for its own sake, as well as a means of creating a more equitable world.

In some respects, the pedagogical approaches adopted by the MFU exist in other areas of civil society, such as book clubs, the University of the Third Age, cafe groups, ideas groups, public seminars and politics in the pub. Even some mainstream universities put on occasional community seminars and conferences where members of the public are invited to engage in public debate – but these are few and far between and I doubt they are organised for entirely altruistic reasons. But it is the dislocation from individualistic values and economic imperatives that most distinguishes these non-mainstream initiatives from the current rationalist trajectories of higher education, as well as their commitment to social change that is relevant to the world in which we live. It's the joy of learning infused with activist purpose.

In the United States, a number of colleges specialising largely in the liberal arts have attempted to give expression to such public virtues – even though, ultimately, they may have been compromised by the market. Colleges such as Bennington, Antioch, Hampshire and Goddard offer programs and courses that enable students to negotiate their desired areas of study. There is much talk of empowerment, collaboration, citizenship, progressive education and what Goddard College refers to as the hoped for 'creative, passionate, and lifelong learners'. This sort of language sounds very appealing, especially for prospective students wanting an education beyond the particular instrumentalism of today's higher education. But there is something strikingly familiar in the commercialised rhetoric that these colleges use. Take for example Antioch College's mission statement:

> Commitment to excellence in scholarship; Commitment to full-time periods in a cooperative work program that alternates with full-time study and supports the link between theory and practice; Commitment to active engagement in the community and to social justice.

Similar mixed bags can be found among other seemingly progressive colleges in America that, in effect, have appropriated both liberal-sounding expressions and the usual corporate mantras of 'excellence' and 'innovation'.

Yet the American liberal arts colleges at least try to deliver courses that recognise the need for an education linked to civic engagement and democratic participation, rather than simply feeding career development and economic growth. They also try to break down some of the barriers to educational participation by avoiding hierarchical assessment approaches like grades. Instead they employ 'narrative evaluations' that convey levels of understanding in an on-going process of participatory learning.

But it is the rationale for the existence of these colleges that so excites, and which bears testimony to their desire to develop a more life-enhancing and rounded approach to education. Here is the president of Benington College, Elizabeth Coleman, talking in 2007 about the need for a 'new liberal arts':

> the vital connection between education, democracy, and a vibrant citizenship – once the bedrock of public education in this country – has atrophied, making the perpetuation of that democracy increasingly precarious ... Civic consciousness and behavior are formed at the intersection of study and engagement – reflection and action – and in public settings where difference and conflict are plentiful and treated as assets, instead of liabilities.

Coleman's view of the atrophying of public education and the need to return tertiary education to 'reflection and action' – indeed, her whole conception of the liberal arts – is thankfully far removed from the 'new humanities' advocated by Australia's Professor Peter Coaldrake. Professor Coleman's views are also shared by countless academics both in the United States and beyond.

Across the Atlantic, the defence against government assaults on the liberal arts in Britain has been led, among others, by the philosopher and serial complainant, AC Grayling. In an article in the *New Statesman* in 2010, Grayling begins by agreeing with the widely held view that British universities are producing 'Disneyland degrees' and that the government treats the humanities as if they were irrelevant to the imperatives of economic activity. But, insists Grayling, this sort of narrow thinking belies the need for comprehensive, imaginative, wide-ranging education that enables people to thrive in a democratic society. After all, he says, society:

> needs its lawyers, journalists, politicians, civil servants, writers, artists and teachers – and it needs everyone on both sides of the science-humanities divide to be a thoughtful voter, good neighbour, loving parent, responsible citizen. In short, society needs to have a civilised conversation with itself about its values and about what is to be learned from the experience of mankind.

Given the concerns over graduates in Australia, it is likely that the Business Council of Australia and Professor Steven Schwartz at Macquarie University would agree with Grayling's views. But the Business Council in particular might not agree with his following broadside delivered in the pages of *The Guardian* in 2009:

> The idea that education is for the mind and soul, for the whole person – the citizen, the parent, the voter, the reader, the lover, the traveller, the human being in the round – is lost to view in trying to make university education a mere continuation of school for the same sausage-machine purpose of churning out employees.

Nor, insists Grayling, is university education about providing students with every supportive prop known to humankind so that they can complete courses: 'University is emphatically not about spoon-feeding and hand-holding through courses, but the very opposite. It is … about autonomy in thinking, researching and writing.'

Unfortunately, with the rise of intensive student support services, designer assessment, and a pass-come-what-may ethos that pervades many universities, the sense of autonomy eulogised by Grayling is a thing of the past. Perhaps this is why the American colleges sound so radical when compared to today's universities: they want students to think for themselves and to be active citizens.. Yes, it could well be that these colleges are also in the commodification game, merely selling another brand that fits the so-called 'radical' agenda. But anything is better than what exists in today's tertiary system.

That said, we need to remain cautious in our pursuit of alternatives. The establishment last year in London of the New College of the Humanities – under the direction of none other than AC Grayling – is a salutary reminder of how an institution initially touted as progressive and alternative to the mainstream turns out to be high-brow and elitist, paying its academic staff more than their counterparts in other tertiary institutions and charging students exorbitant fees – the latter going some way to subsiding the former.

Moral pragmatism

While paradigm-busters might offer some splendid alternatives to what exists in today's higher education system, the fact remains that the majority of academics have to work *within* the current system – if only to pay off the mortgage and feed the kids. Much as I am highly suspicious of pragmatism and pragmatists, I think there is a case, at least in the short to medium term, for negotiating meaningful intellectual and activist spaces within the current university framework. Indeed, many academics have already sought to do so over the years. This is far from easy, but with some covert subversion, resistance and the odd reforms and strategic victories it may be possible to make academic life a little more bearable – and even lay the foundations for a different approach to higher education.

But what I am about to suggest carries risks in the form of failure to secure promotion, hostile faculty management and sneers from your compromised colleagues. By undermining or questioning the current regime, even in the most innocuous of ways, and seeking to promote the idea of academic work as vital to a meaningful democracy, an academic is bound to attract the ire of others, especially if certain actions threaten the brand.

I asked one senior scholar from the ANU what he might say to a troubled, questioning academic.

'I would advise most academics to try and survive as best you can, be careful what you say and try and teach the examined life as best you can.'

I thought that sounded a bit tame, tantamount to tacitly supporting the current system, but then he added:

> I'd tell the buggers to look for another job, because being an academic in today's university system means that the life of the mind is being utterly undermined. I think it is irresponsible to encourage anyone into academic life.

'What would lead to a major change in the system?', I inquired.

> Well, you have to start with the view that the system as it stands is a manifest failure. It doesn't deliver high-quality education or rounded students, far from it. Just look at business graduates! If the [vice chancellors] had any gumption, any belief that higher education should be about genuine critical reflection, dialogue and social concern they would have taken the government on by mounting a very public debate over under-funding. They could have used their funds to put a great big advertisement out there. That at least would have told the public that all is not

> right in the university sector. Instead they have gone along with the system; yes, they moaned about underfunding, but helped turn universities into factories. What we need is a catastrophe, a meltdown of the system to demonstrate to the public what universities are all about. The VCs can speak the language of academic freedom, higher education and all that, but academics in the system, most of us, know what a load of crap that is.

But what specifically can academics do to make life more meaningful and tolerable? How can or should they stay in a system that seems so manifestly antithetical to academics' interests and well being? After much reflection and umpteen conversations with my academic complainants, I have come up with a few suggestions as to how academics can best navigate the troubled waters of their daily professional existence and retain some sense that they are in control of their situations and doing something toward the common good. I offer these suggestions as an adjunct to the ongoing struggle to engage various audiences through public and policy discourses:

- As a matter of principle, constantly contest the standardised, rigidified, mechanised approach to teaching and keep faith with the examined life.
- Help push for the infusion of civic and democratised 'wisdom' into higher education by insisting that arts, social sciences and humanities are core to a rounded education.
- Link pedagogy to action, and remember the following dictum: Multinational corporations have commodified everything; the point is to always expose this.
- Routinely reframe language by referring to social capital, citizenship, participatory democracy, community, public

education, students rather than consumers, dialogue and debate rather than inputs, outputs and impacts; and social activism and the collective good rather than product or career.

- Make sure that your assessment items include direct student contact with social groups and community organisations.
- Place routine critical inquiry with students, colleagues and others at the forefront of your pedagogical being.
- Contribute to radical, alternative, progressive, activist educational approaches outside the sphere of current tertiary influence. (Call this 'community engagement' if need be.)
- Turn every corporatised item raised at meetings into the subject of critical discussion.
- Resist the temptation to disengage from key committees. Senior academics should seek to include deconstructivist principles at academic board, curriculum and other committees. If on a promotions panel, you should ask searching questions of those candidates who have devoted their careers to administration and income generation. Always closely inspect the research and publications records of all candidates, especially their contribution to civil society.
- Consult with teaching and learning personnel, but on most occasions simply ignore their recommendations. (Never patronise them, however, as they have links with heads of school and deans.)
- Do research and consultancies that build alliances with oppressed, marginalised and disempowered groups. Submit grant applications that promote this aim.
- Engage students in discussions about learning, citizenship and participatory democracy, and invite them to consider the role of universities in this respect.
- Encourage students to critically evaluate the system of student evaluations of units.

- Organise seminars and small conferences that tackle major issues of the day. Invite members of the public to attend and refer to this as a 'town and gown initiative'. (Vice chancellors like this sort of rhetoric.)
- Hold regular morning and afternoon teas and lunches with coll-eagues and discuss what makes higher education 'higher', and find common areas of complaint and relate this to forms of ameliorative action. Employ this as a mechanism for building alliances.
- Contribute regularly to Unileaks.
- Seek to include students in most aspects of decision-making, especially in relation to course content and assessment.
- Constantly bring up the issue of casuals and sessional employment, relate this to what is taught in units (social justice, human rights etc.) and talk with the casuals and sessionals about them joining a union.
- If confronted about any of the above by faculty managers or para-academic apparatchiks, argue that what you are doing is in the interests of 'cost-effectiveness' and 'income generation'.
- Join the NTEU, build on its many achievements.
- Remember that sleeping in, enjoying your evenings and weekends are acts of resistance in the neo-liberal university.
- When on university grounds, always have a briefcase with papers hanging out and look breathless. This will make you appear busy and therefore less of a focus for managerial attention. Never read books on campus, since this is considered a waste of time.
- When reading articles in the main higher education outlets, see most of them for what they are: props for the establishment. Use this material in your classes, and get students to deconstruct them from a critical perspective.

- If you haven't got a sense of humour, develop one. You'll need it.

Applied in small, discrete doses, such actions may help you create the time and space you need for progressive academic work and joyfully but constructively undermine the system at the same time. Some of your students might thank you for enabling them to think beyond an individualistic ethos. You might even take a few of your colleagues along for the ride – consider this as part of an exercise aimed at airing common grievances. Give it a go: make up your own bucket list. The last thing you should do is retreat to your office and get depressed or listen to songs of rebellion by long-lost folk singers. If nothing else, the things you have learnt or are already aware of about Whackademia will provide you with the know-how to survive and thrive. It's worth a go, and it's better than simply waiting for something to happen.

Conclusion: Seeing through Whackademia

Can you honestly imagine Ludwig Wittgenstein, Hannah Arendt or Ivan Illich as lecturers in one of Australia's universities? They'd be constantly under the heel of line managers for having refused to go along with the university's strategic plan, and they certainly wouldn't be promoted because they wouldn't have done enough committee work or administration. You'd have Wittgenstein ending his career on the third rung of the Lecturer B scale in some dingy office because all he'd do was sit around contemplating ideas and writing stuff. 'What about doing some course co-ordination and chairing a few meetings', his colleagues would insist. He'd flunk every performance review because he'd question the rationale for the process and probably fail to turn up.

SENIOR LECTURER IN POLITICAL SCIENCE, MELBOURNE

While this book presents a number of critical insights into the strange world of Australian higher education, especially through the experiences of academics, it is important to restate that, despite all their current oddities, universities manage to produce some good, interesting and civically useful teaching, research and community service. But much of this is achieved in spite of, not because of, the current policies and practices of these institutions.

If the tertiary system was transformed to meet the needs of civil society rather than just the economy, if it was concerned more with what it means to be a 'rounded', active, democratic citizen rather than a consumer, and if it truly allowed for academic autonomy and freedom, then more enlightened, engaged and civically relevant work would surely ensue. We might even produce more prominent and passionate public intellectuals speaking their minds about issues like Australia's treatment of refugees, the Palestine–Israel question, climate change, animal rights, war and peace, global poverty, hunger, corporate greed, economic growth, the steady state – even the corporatisation of universities!

Moreover, instead of hearing about career options and the potential for high salaries and material accumulation, our graduates might contemplate issues and ideas around their spiritual and emotional needs. They might even prefer to end up working in a community garden or food co-operative rather than an investment bank. Rather than the credentialised euphoria that currently greets graduation, our students might be better prepared to live a more fulfilled and altruistic life, and develop a sense of the collective human experience. Unfortunately, as things stand, neo-liberal ideologues, blinkered policy-makers and bureaucrats now run the show, meaning that we are likely to see a continuation of policies that position universities primarily as feeders for the economy.

Whatever position we take in relation to the current state of higher education, it is clear that over recent decades there has been a confluence of ideological and political forces that have resulted in the creation of Whackademia – a strange, over-regulated and repressive culture that makes free, socially relevant, impassioned and truly critical academic work difficult. Why? Because the creation of a powerful bureaucratic and heavily regulated system, linked predominantly to productivist concerns, has led to many negative effects, many of which work against the idea of universities as places of vibrant scholarship. Given the creation of a marketised system, with all its compromised, commercial shallowness, universities were always likely to suffer a decline in autonomy, intellectual integrity, standards and civic purpose.

Not surprisingly in such a context, academics are required, preferably as docile conformists, to toe the corporate line and to do everything in their power to attract and retain students, as well as promote the corporate brand. Inevitably, this approach to university governance – evidenced in the pronouncements of vice chancellors, government ministers and policy advisers – has had an enormous impact on the day-to-day experiences of academics. Some, especially those in the elite universities, have a better time of it than say, those in regional outposts, but no-one escapes the systemic befuddlement and eternal managerial gaze that is Whackademia.

What unites the vast majority of academics I have spoken to is not simply a litany of complaints, but rather a sense of dismay about how the university system has been degraded, as well as the hope that a different system may emerge – one more sympathetic to the intrinsic value of education and its contribution to a truly democratic society. Most academics complain not because they want to bring the system down – although a lot do – or because they have a preferred ideology, but because they care deeply about their own role as educators and researchers. They feel that the effects of recent policy and organisational changes have dramatically altered various power relations within universities and, by extension, the way they govern and organise themselves. Many argue that universities were in many respects better for academics in the pre-Dawkins era, when the educational process was more collegial and less competitive and instrumental than in today's system. I don't think these views can or should be easily dismissed.

Then again, supporters of today's system might argue that at least academics are participating in a more open and democratic system of mass education. While it cannot be denied that there are and will be more students than ever before in the system, academics remain seriously concerned about what they see as a decline in standards, both in terms of the lowering of expectations in certain disciplines and by implication, the 'dumbing down' of actual content. Again, these sorts of views should not be disregarded.

Perhaps academics' most severe criticisms are reserved for senior university management, the members of which many academics regard as compromised by large salary packages and devoid of any serious questioning of the higher education system – other than complaining about the lack of federal government funding. There are of course exceptions to this rule, but they are few and far between. Most academics I have spoken to referred to the parallel universes that seem to co-exist in the sector, with government ministers and vice chancellors publicly extolling the virtues of higher education while academics complain bitterly about the very opposite. Interestingly, in the great 'republic of learning' which, according to Professor Glyn Davis, is the massified tertiary system, academics barely warrant a mention – unless of course they have been awarded a Nobel Prize, obtained a large grant and/or a teaching award. Rarely do vice chancellors publicly acknowledge, let alone take seriously, the many grievances raised by academics.

Recently I heard philosopher John Armstrong proposing a change to the humanities. He was arguing against the claimed intrinsic value of disciplines that exist under the umbrella of humanities, and for a higher form of value that enables an active engagement with the wider community by breaking down elitist institutional barriers and cultivating 'dispositions' that are applicable to 'real-world situations'. On the surface this seems a position I could support, but these 'dispositions' and 'real-life situations' remain something of a mystery, as does Armstrong's conception of the world in which we live. Armstrong suggests, more or less, that those in humanities who seek to defend their disciplines are a bit stuffy and antiquated, lacking in self-reflection. He maintains that disciplines need to be opened up to make them relevant to everyday concerns. But, one might ask, which specific concerns? What about global poverty, inequality, hunger, war and so forth? Are these integral to 'everyday' concerns? Armstrong even suggests that non-academics should be part of the refereeing process of academic articles, and perhaps sit on university committees – which of course raises more questions than answers.

Despite Armstrong's attempts at social inclusion, what he seems to forget when talking about the humanities is the context within which the relevant disciplines operate, and why academics might be defensive. After all, the constriction of the humanities in Britain, the assault on various disciplines in Australia and elsewhere, the under-funding, casualisation and under-staffing of humanities courses, and the promotion of what former chair of Universities Australia, Professor Peter Coaldrake, refers to as the 'new humanities' would make any humanities scholar a touch nervous. Armstrong also seems oblivious to the commercial imperative of the university sector and its links to the economy, GDP, and notions of 'progress' and 'growth' – the latter of which belongs to the terrain of what Professor John Quiggan regards as 'zombie economics'.

But perhaps the most significant omission in Armstrong's analysis is the tertiary sector's obsession with brand protection and income generation. This impacts on just about everything that goes on inside our higher education institutions. If the brand is the life-blood of today's tertiary system, and if a demand-led system means that certain disciplines, courses and units have to go to the wall, then so be it. Frederick Hayek, exponent of the unfettered market and 'spontaneous order', would surely be elated by such developments. In failing to address such matters, Armstrong's critique of humanities and his genuine desire for greater public openness, flexibility and engagement ends up – inadvertently perhaps – supporting the very system of which he is a part, and by the same token, giving plenty of ammunition to the compromised critics of humanities. After all, Armstrong's current position – Philosopher in Residence at the Melbourne Business School and senior adviser to the vice chancellor of Melbourne University – suggests he may not be such an objective critic.

If vice chancellors and government ministers want advice on where universities might go from here, they could do worse than canvass the views of Australia's academics. There are hordes of very qualified advisers among the academic workforce, yet their opinions – especially of the more 'radical' persuasion – seem to have been largely ignored by policy-makers and university chiefs. But their opinions are definitely out there. Take the open letter by over a hundred senior academics ('Academics Australia') to newly elected prime minister Kevin Rudd in 2007. In addition to noting the 'widespread demoralisation' of academics, they put forward a number of policy suggestions which could lift the higher education sector out of its current doldrums. Their key suggestions were:

- Slim down and simplify the requirements of the higher education bureaucracy, and thus reduce university administrative costs
- Provide world-class university education for our future generations through full government funding for the sector's teaching-related expenditures – including education at the honours and postgraduate levels
- Reduce universities' dependence on overseas full-fee students – a practice that has led to the emergence of cash-crop education programs that have damaged Australia's reputation in education; and
- Revive Australian universities' faltering international standing in innovative research by increasing funding for competitive research projects in all areas.

Unfortunately, these eminently sensible proposals from a cross-section of academic heavyweights have been roundly ignored by the federal government. It's not surprising, therefore, that other demoralised academics see little hope in halting the juggernaut that is marketised tertiary education. In effect, academics have been rendered the unpeople of the university system – their voices largely ignored, their autonomy and their freedom limited, every activity monitored, and their work regarded as relevant only by virtue of its capacity to obtain grants and get students through the system. This has led to an enforced acquiescence, disengagement from and smouldering resistance to the prevailing order and, in some cases, utter hopelessness and resignation.

Given what I have heard from academics, it is patently obvious that most do not view universities as great places to work. Vice chancellors will of course argue that there is some great work going on in the sector and I would agree with them. But I would also argue that their failure to take on board the concerns of academics and to engage the public in a debate about what university education is for, to have acquiesced so meekly to the particular instrumental priorities set by government, and to have compromised standards has led to a system less than worthy of the label 'higher education'. Additionally, in a world confronted by the great challenges of climate change, shifts to new ways of living, opposition to corporate greed and global inequality, Australian and other Western universities, with their blinkered support for neo-liberal agendas, run the very real risk of total irrelevance.

For those academics waiting for change there are, as noted in the previous chapter, a number of practical things they can do to create meaningful space for themselves within an over-regulated and highly bureaucratised system. They can begin identifying common ground with their colleagues, administrators and students; they can argue for change, and propose and articulate new visions of higher education outside the current system. All this takes time, effort, courage, and active engagement with colleagues, as well as participation in trade unions, non-government organisations, and the general public. It means also squaring off what we teach with what we do, and never letting oppressive practices go by without a complaint – complaint with purpose. Purposeful complaint is of course already widespread among academics and other sectors of the tertiary workforce, the task now is to broaden and strengthen the scope of the struggle against neo-liberal university education.

None of this is easy. It simply isn't possible to down tools and strategise all day: we do require a certain level of moral pragmatism just to get by. But although many academics in the current system are fearful of speaking out about university life – evidenced in the fact that only a handful of my respondents agreed to partially identify themselves and their institutions – there is nonetheless a strong desire for change. The first steps to venturing beyond survival mode are engagement and dialogue, practices that should include those who are happy as things are. The alternative is simply to retreat behind closed doors and carry on moaning and groaning, proceed regardless, pretend that it really doesn't matter, or quietly retire.

It's not much of a choice when you come to think about it. But at the heart of our thoughts and actions should be the question: what kind of university culture would we like to be a part of, and what role should universities play in the general order of things? These are big questions with no easy answers, but they are nevertheless worth a decent public airing.

References and further reading

A considerable amount of information for this book was drawn from articles contained in newspapers, newsletters, academic journals and magazines. I found *The Australian*'s 'Higher Education' supplement, *Campus Review*, *Australian Universities Review*, *Journal of Higher Education*, *Policy and Management*, and the National Tertiary Education Union's *Advocate* particularly useful in charting the changes sweeping over the Australian higher education sector. I also drew on blogs and information contained on federal government, university, union and other websites. Below I list some of the more salient of these sources, as well as a number of books dealing either directly or tangentially with higher education both here and overseas.

ABC Radio National (2009), *The Science Show*, ABC Radio, www.abc.net.au/rn/scienceshow/stories/2009/2515761.htm

Academics Australia (2007), Open letter to the Australian Prime Minister, the Hon Kevin Rudd, calling for revolution in higher education, www.academics-australia.org

Access Economics (2011), *Broader Implications from a Downturn in International Students*, 30 June, www.universitiesaustralia.edu.au/resources/618/1100

The Age (2010), 'Third degree', 28 May, blogs.theage.com.au/thirddegree/archives/2010/05/apathy_rules.html

Alexander, H (2007) 'When business pulls up a chair', *Sydney Morning Herald*, 13 March

—— (2010) 'Places to eat and work give students plenty of staying power', *Sydney Morning Herald*, 3 Jan

Andrew, M (2007), 'Why business must engage with universities', *The Age*, 31 Aug

—— (2011) 'Companies must support and guide education sector', *The Australian*, 'Higher Education', 2 April

Antioch College (2011), 'Mission', antiochcollege.org/about/

Armstrong, J (2011), 'Reformation and renaissance: New life for the humanities?', *Saturday Extra*, ABC Radio, 5 Feb, www.abc.net.au/rn/saturdayextra/stories/2011/3129929.htm

—— (2011), 'Reformation and renaissance', *Griffith Review*, www.griffithreview.com/edition-31-ways-of-seeing/reformation-and-renaissance

Arum, R, and Roksa, J (2011), *Academically Adrift: Limited Learning on College Campuses*, Chicago: University of Chicago Press

Australian Council for Educational Research (2011), *Australasian Survey of Student Engagement*, www.acer.edu.au/research/ausse

Australian Research Council (2010), *Excellence in Research for Australia*, www.arc.gov.au/pdf/ERA_s1.pdf

—— (2011), 'Ranked outlets', www.arc.gov.au/era/era_journal_list.htm#1

Baggini, J (2010), *Complaint: From Minor Moans to Principled Protests*, London: Profile Books

Barrie, S, Ginns, P, and Symons, R (2008), *Final Report: Student Surveys on Teaching and Learning*, Australian Learning and Teaching Council, www.altc.edu.au/system/files/App%2011%20Student_Surveys_on_Teaching_and_Learning-Final_Report_for%20PDF_0.pdf

Beardy, L (2010), 'Schwartz paints picture of "moral zombification" amongst graduates', *Campus Review*, 20(17), p 8

Beljac, M (2009), 'What ails Australia's universities?', *On-line Opinion*, 12 August, www.onlineopinion.com.au/view.asp?article=9285

Bennett, J (2011), 'Formal letter was university's answer to plea for help', *Campus Review*, 21(15), p 4

Betts, K, and Birrell, B (2010), 'Editorial', *People and Place*, 18(4)

Bexley, E, James, R and Arkoudis, S (2011), *The Australian Academic*

Profession in Transition: Addressing the Challenge of Reconceptualising Academic Work and Regenerating the Academic Workforce, Centre for the Study of Higher Education, University of Melbourne, www.cshe.unimelb.edu.au/people/bexley_docs/The_Academic_Profession_in_Transition_Sept2011.pdf

Biggs, J, and Davis, R (eds) (2002), *The Subversion of Australian Universities*, Wollongong: Fund for Intellectual Dissent

Blackmore, J (2011), 'Student satisfaction: Is this the only meaningful measure of quality teaching', *Campus Review*, 21(2), pp 10–11

Blackwell, A (2011), 'Barber's dream university in cyberspace', *Campus Review*, 21(12), p 11

Boyer, D (2010), *The Republic of Learning and the 2010 Boyer Lectures*, ABC on-line, 18 June, www.abc.net.au/corp/pubs/media/s2933346.htm

Bradley, D, Noonan, P, Nugent, H, and Scales, B (2008), *Review of Australian Higher Education: Final Report*, Canberra: Commonwealth of Australia www.deewr.gov.au/HigherEducation/Review/Documents/PDF/Higher%20Education%20Review_one%20document_02.pdf

Brown, M (2010), 'Foreign student drop leads to uni job cuts', *ABC News*, 14 October. www.abc.net.au/news/stories/2010/10/14/3037834.htm

Brown, T, Goodman, J, and Keiko, Y (2010), 'Academic casualisation in Australia: Class divisions in the University', *Journal of Industrial Relations*, 52(2), pp 169–82

Brown, T, Goodman, J, and Yasukwa, K (2008), 'Casualisation of academic work: Industrial justice and quality education', *Academy of the Social Sciences*, 27(1), pp 17–29

Carty, T (2008), 'Uni chief's new BMW before ICAC', *Sydney Morning Herald*, 7 Sept

Carvini, E (2000), 'If the slogan fits', *The Age*, 25 Sept

Coaldrake, P (2010), 'The higher education revolution: Great ambition, challenging realities', National Press Club, 4 March, www.npc.org.au/speakerarchive/professor-peter-coaldrake.html

—— (2011), 'A tricky balancing act', *The Australian*, 'Higher Education', 18 May, p 29

Coates, H, and Goedegebuure, L (2010), 'The real Academic revolution: Why we need to reconceptualise Australia's future academic workforce, and eight possible strategies for how to go about this', Research briefing, LH Martin Institute

Coates, H, Dobson, I, Edwards, D, Friedman, T, Goedegebuure, L and Meek, L (2009), *The Attractiveness of the Australian Academic Profession: A Comparative Analysis*, LH Martin Institute, www.lhmartininstitute.edu.au/userfiles/files/research/attractiveness_ac_prof_res_brief.pdf

Coates, H, Dobson, IR, Goedegebuure, L, and Meek, L (2009), 'Australia's casual approach to its academic teaching workforce', *People and Place*, 17(4), pp 47–54

Coleman, E (2007), 'The Bennington curriculum: A new liberal art', 6 Oct, www.

bennington.edu/go/about-bennington/a-new-liberal-arts
The Conversation (2011), 'Lost international student enrolments may cost Australia billions', 6 July, theconversation.edu.au/lost-international-student-enrolments-may-cost-australia-billions-2199
Cooper, D (2011), 'New rules for success on the tertiary playing field', *Campus Review*, 21(19), pp 10–11
Cooper, S (2011), 'With friends like John Armstrong ...', *Arena Magaizine*, 13, pp 54–55
Cooper, S, and Poletti, A (2011), 'The new ERA of journal ranking: The consequences of Australia's fraught encounter with quality', *Australian Universities Review*, 53(1)
Cowley, J (2010), 'Confronting the reality of casualisation in Australia: Recognising difference and embracing sessional staff in law schools', *QUT Law Journal*, 10(1)
Davis, G (2011), *The Republic of Learning: Higher Education Transforms Australia*, Canberra: ABC Books
Davis, L (2010), '10 Weird and wonderful university courses', *Independent News*, www.independent.co.uk/news/education/education-news/10-weird-and-wonderful-university-courses-2074911.html
Dawkins, J (1987), *Higher Education: A Policy Discussion Paper*, Department of Employment, Education and Training, Canberra: Australian Government Publishing Service
—— (1988), *Higher Education: A Policy Statement*, Canberra: Australian Government Publishing Service
Department of Education, Employment and Workplace Relations (2010), *Staff 2010: Selected Higher Education Statistics; Number of Full-time and Fractional Full-time Staff by Current Duties Term, 1996 to 2010*, Canberra: Commonwealth of Australia
—— (2010), *2009 Higher Education Student Statistics*, www.deewr.gov.au/HigherEducation/Pages/Overview.aspx
Dobson, I (2011), quoted in A McGilvray, 'Lobbying and late changes to journal rankings', *Campus Review*, 21(6), p 3
Eagleton, T (2011), 'AC Grayling's private university is odious', *The New Significance*, 7 June, www.thenewsignificance.com/2011/06/07/terry-eagleton-ac-graylings-private-university-is-odious
English, T (2011), 'Weasel words and the soft sell', *The Australian*, 'Higher Education', March 16
Evans, G (2011), quoted in S Woodward, 'Carr's research message falls on some skeptical ears', *Campus Review*, 21(4), p 9
Featherstone, T (2011), 'Does university business education still pay?', *The Age*, 14 Feb
Fry, T (2010), *The Fry Chronicles: An Autobiography*, London: Michael Joseph
Furedi, F (2006), *Where Have All the Intellectuals Gone?*, London: Continuum Press
—— (2009), *Wasted: Why Education Isn't Educating*, London: Continuum Press

—— (2011) 'Introduction', in Molesworth et al (eds), *The Marketisation of Higher Education and the Student as Consumer*, London: Routledge
Gaita, R (2007), 'Betrayed by utilitarianism?', *The Australian*, July 14
Gare, S (2006), *Triumph of the Airheads and the Retreat from Commonsense*, Paris: Maine, Park Street Press
Gilmore, H (2010), 'No time for playtime', *Sydney Morning Herald*, 15 May
—— (2010), 'Pay packets head to $1m but academics left behind', *Sydney Morning Herald*, 5 June
Goddard College (2011), Mission statement, www.goddard.edu/mission
Gora, J (2009), 'Have you finished your marking?', *Campus Review*, 7 July
—— (2009), 'Is there hope for the unit information guide?', *Campus Review*, 6 April
—— (2009), 'No time for time management', *Campus Review*, 8 Feb
—— (2009), 'Sorry, I'm too busy', *Campus Review*, 27 July
—— (2010), 'Are you going to the staff meeting?', *Campus Review*, 16 May
—— (2010), 'Fodder factories won't do', *The Australian*, 'Higher Education', 15 Sept
—— (2010), 'It's great to be a slow learner', *The Australian*, 'Higher Education', 27 Oct
—— (2010), 'Run that sexy motto by me again', *Australian Universities Review*, 52(1), pp 77–80
—— (2010), 'Watch out! Here comes the TEQSA juggernaut', *Australian Universities Review*, 52(2)
—— (2011), 'We'll support you ever more!', *Australian Universities Review*, 53(1)
Gora, J, and Whelan, A (2010), 'Invasion of the aca-zombies', *The Australian*, 'Higher Education', 3 Nov
Gosling, D (2008), *Survey of Directors of Academic Development in Australian Universities: Final Report*, www.swinburne.edu.au/spl/awardsgrants/recipients/dahef/files/Survey%20of%20Directors%20of%20Academic%20Development%20in%20Australian%20Universities.pdf
Gottschalk, L (2007), *Casual and Sessional Employment: Motivation and Work/life Balance*, Ballarat, University of Ballarat Business School, www.ballarat.edu.au/ard/business/resources/casual_sessional_employ.pdf
Graduate Careers Australia, website, (www.graduatecareers.com.au)
Grayling, AC (2009), 'Universities are not there to spoon-feed', *The Guardian*, 10 Nov, www.guardian.co.uk/commentisfree/2009/nov/10/university-contact-hours-mandelson
—— (2010), 'Universities challenged', *New Statesman*, 26 October, www.newstatesman.com/education/2010/10/humanities-training-needs
Hare, J (2010), 'Vice Chancellor Steven Schwartz delves into the wise and wherefores', *The Australian*, 'Higher Education', 1 Sept
—— (2010) 'High university drop-out rates cost $1.4bn', *The Australian*, 'Higher Education', 20 Oct
—— (2011), 'Elite eight head university research ratings', *The Australian*,

'Higher Education', 31 Jan
—— (2011), 'Most universities below par on research', *The Australian*, 'Higher Education', 1 Feb
—— (2011), 'Business takes dim view of academe', *The Australian*, 'Higher Education', 30 March, p 29
—— (2011), 'Researcher slams secretive science', *The Australian*, 'Higher Education', 8 June, p 37
—— (2011), 'Academics face looming crisis', *The Australian*, 'Higher Education', 21 Sept, p 27
Hare, J, and Trounson, A (2011), 'ERA lays bare research myths', *The Australian*, 'Higher Education', 2 February
Harrison, D (2011), 'Growth in uni places good for the economy, says Labor', *Sydney Morning Herald*, 22 April, p 9
Hawken, P (2008), *Blessed Unrest: How the Largest Social Movement in History is Restoring Grace, Justice, and Beauty to the World*, New York: Penguin
Hil, R, and Eddy, E (eds) (2002), *Beyond the Enterprise University*, NTEU/University of Sunshine Coast
Hilzinger, K (2011), 'Does university business education still pay?', *The Age*, 14 Feb
Holt, S (2010), 'How Google is killing higher education', *Technorati*, 19 October, technorati.com/technology/article/how-google-is-killing-higher-education
Jones, P (1997), 'Why I'm off', *Spectator*, 279(88)
Junor, A (2004), 'Casual university work: Choice risk and equity and the case for regulation', *Economics and Labour Review*, 14(2), pp 276–304
Kayrooz, C, Kinnear, P, and Preston, P (2001), *Academic Freedom and Commercialisation of Australian Universities: Perceptions and Experiences of Social Scientists*, Australia Institute, www.tai.org.au/documents/dp_fulltext/DP37.pdf
Klein, N (2000), *No Logo: Taking Aim at the Brand Bullies*, New York: Knopf
Lane, B (2011), 'Slump in Chinese students begins', *The Australian*, 'Higher Education', 4 May, p 34
—— (2011), 'My Uni ready to test in July', *The Australian*, 'Higher Education', 25 May, p 25
—— (2011), 'International students see Australia as "a shop rather than cultural bridge"', *The Australian*, 'Higher Education', 7 Sept, p 27
—— (2011), 'Rise in teaching-only positions bucks tradition', *The Australian*, 'Higher Education', 16 Nov, p 30
Larkins, F (2011), *University Discipline Diversity Matters for Research Excellence*, LH Martin Institute, 28 Sept, www.lhmartininstitute.edu.au/insights-blog/2011/09/60-university-discipline-diversity-matters-for-research-excellence
Livingstone, T (2007), 'QUT drops humanities', *Courier Mail*, 21 April
MacCallum, M (2001), *The Man Who Laughs*, ABC Audio
McGhee, M (2010), 'A university's soul is its freedom of ideas', *Guardian*, 18 Oct

Macfarlane, B (2007), *The Academic Citizen: The Virtue of Service in University Life*, New York: Routledge
McWilliams, E (2002), *How to Survive Best Practice*, Sydney: UNSW Press
Marginson, S (2011), 'The public rationale of the universities', *Dissent*, 36, Spring, pp 26–31
Marginson, S, and Considine, M (2000), *The Enterprise University: Power, Governance and Reinvention in Australia*, Oakleigh: Cambridge University Press
Martin, B (2009), 'Academic patronage', *International Journal for Educational Integrity*, 5(1), pp 3–19
Massaro, V (2009), 'Unpacking the Bradley report', *The Australian*, 'Higher Education', 17 Feb
Matchett, S (2008) 'Teaching load carried by "servants"', *The Australian*, 'Higher Education', 25 June
Melbourne Free University (2011), website, melbournefreeuniversity.org
Middleton, S (2011), 'Never mind the score, look at the result', *Campus Review*, 221(21), p 16
Molesworth, M, Scullipon, R, and Nixon, E (eds) (2011), *The Marketisation of Higher Education and the Student as Consumer*, London: Routledge
Moodie, G (2011), 'Areas below world class at greater risk', *The Australian*, 'Higher Edcuation', 2 Feb
Narushima, Y (2011), 'When universities go begging', *Sydney Morning Herald*, 30 April–1 May, p 6
—— (2011), 'Universities should "trade in morals not profits"', *Sydney Morning Herald*, 6 June, p 5
—— (2011), 'Universities look for benefactors to close funding gap', *Sydney Morning Herald*, 21 June
National Tertiary Education Union (2009), *Overload: The Role of Work Role Escalation and Micro-management of Work Patterns in Loss of Morale and Collegiality at UWS: The Way Forward*, Sydney: NTEU
—— (2011), 'NTEU survey reveals CSU staff are overworked to the point of illness', 17 October, www.nteu.org.au/article/NTEU-survey-reveals-CSU-staff-are-overworked-to-the-point-of-illness-12025
—— (2011), 'Well-funded public universities critical for Australia future', www.nteu.org.au/library/view/id/1665
Nussbaum, M (2010), *Not for Profit: Why Democracy Needs the Humanities*, Princeton: Princeton University Press
O'Neil, A (2010), 'Reach for the stars', *Australian Universities Review*, 52
Parker, S (2010), 'Markets and missions', *Campus Review*, 20(17), p 12
Polya, G (1999), 'Gagging academics: Death of the university? An open letter to the Council of La Trobe University', www.bmartin.cc/dissent/documents/Austunispeak/LaTrobe1999_08.html
—— (2001), 'Crisis in our universities', *Ockham's Razor*, ABC Radio, 19 August, www.abc.net.au/rn/science/ockham/stories/s347931.htm
Professor X (2011), *In the Basement of the Ivory Tower: Confessions of an*

Accidental Academic, Viking
Quiggan, J (2010), *Zombie Economics: How Dead Ideas Still Walk Among Us*, Princeton: Princeton University Press
Rangott, M (2011), 'Bargaining outcomes for women', *Agenda*, 10, Sept, p 14
Richardson, S, and Friedman, T (2010), *Australian Regional Higher Education: Student Characteristics and Experiences*, Australian Council for Educational Research, www.deewr.gov.au/HigherEducation/Documents/AusRegionHigherEd-StudentCharExp.pdf
Rosenberg, J (2012), 'Uni caught out trying to poach students using private data base', *Sydney Morning Herald*, 6 Jan, p 1
—— (2012), 'University off the hook over architecture poaching', *Sydney Morning Herald*, 7 Jan, p 3
—— (2011), 'Voices will be silenced if boards are cut, say students', *Sydney Morning Herald*, 20 Oct, p 5
Ross, J (2011), 'Prudential model for TESQA: Bradley', *Campus Review*, 20(6), p 9
—— (2011), 'Rankings do more harm than good', *The Australian*, 'Higher Education', 17 June
Rowbotham, J (2010), 'Casual numbers blow out', *The Australian*, 'Higher Education', 8 Dec
—— (2010), 'Casuals data hides reality on staff workloads', *The Australian*, 'Higher Education', 15 Dec
—— (2011), 'Employer call for English fluency', *The Australian*, 'Higher Education', 12 Jan
—— (2011), 'Unis must brace for ERA funding consequences', *The Australian*, 'Higher Education', 16 Feb
—— (2011), 'Tactical moves ahead of ERA II', *The Australian*, 'Higher Education', 16 March
—— (2011), 'Journal rankings don't reflect performance', *The Australian*, 'Higher Education', 20 March
—— (2011), 'Postgrads shy away from unis', *The Australian*, 'Higher Education', 4 May, p 37
—— (2011), 'Carr bows to rank rebellion', *The Australian*, 'Higher Education', 1 June, p 25
—— (2011), '$6.9m bequest a lifeline to Sydney archaeologists', *The Australian*, 'Higher Education', 29 June, p 34
—— (2011), 'Staff vent their fears to NTEU', *The Australian*, 'Higher Education', 3 August, p 30
—— (2011), 'Student-staff ratios ballooning', *The Australian*, 'Higher Education', 2 Nov, p 21
Rowe, D, and Barnes, K (2008), 'Praise the brand and pass the gag', *The Australian*, 'Higher Education', 18 June, p 28
Schwartz, S (2011), 'The getting of wisdom', *On-Line Opinion*, 13 July, www.onlineopinion.com.au/view.asp?article=12312
—— (2011), 'Little wisdom in narrow learning', *The Australian*, 'Higher

Education', 8 Sept
Shah, M, and Nair, C (2011), *Employer Satisfaction of University Graduates: Key Capabilities in Early Career Graduates*, Teaching and Learning Forum, otl.curtin.edu.au/tlf/tlf2011/refereed/shah.html
Strathern, M (2000), *Audit Cultures: Anthropological Studies in Accountability, Ethics and the Academy*, London: European Association of Social Anthropologists/Routledge
Tanner, L (2011), *Sideshow: Dumbing Down Democracy*, Melbourne: Scribe Publications
—— (2011), 'Universities must adapt or die in the e-learning world', *The Australian*, 'Higher Education', 26 Oct, p 31
Taylor, L (2011), 'A concluding comment from the Vice Chancellor of Poppleton University', in Molesworth et al (eds), *The Marketisation of Higher Education and the Student as Consumer*, London: Routledge
Taylor, S (2004), 'Researching progressive scholarship in Australian universities', in Hil and Eddy (eds), *Beyond the Enterprise University*
Travers, M (2011), *The New Bureaucracy: Quality Assurance and its Critics*, Cambridge: Policy Press
—— (2011), 'Letter to the Editor', *The Australian*, 'Higher Education', 13 April, p 28
Trounson, A (2011), 'On-line is not a substitute for face-to-face teaching', *The Australian*, 'Higher Education', 9 March
—— (2011), 'Free ride past language barrier', *The Australian*, 'Higher Education', 16 March
—— (2011), 'La Trobe solution "divisive"', *The Australian*, 'Higher Education', 20 April, p 22
—— (2011), 'Universities fail because of a lack of faith in the truth', *The Australian*, 'Higher Education', 27 April, p 18
—— (2011), 'Mass university sector is unsustainable', *The Australian*, 'Higher Education', 4 May, p 38
—— (2011),'Standing up for the humanities', *The Australian*, 'Higher Education', 29 June, p 37
—— (2011), 'Overseas students "get soft pass marks"', *The Australian*, 'Higher Education', 2 Nov, p 21
—— (2011), 'Student numbers grow, but not English language support', *The Australian*, 'Higher Education', 9 Nov, p 27
—— (2011), 'Unis eye debt as surplus rises 8pc', *The Australian*, 'Higher Education', 16 Nov, p 27
Universities Australia (2011), website, www.universitiesaustralia.edu.au/page/australia-s-universities
University of Tasmania (2011), 'Student Evaluation of Teaching and Learning' (webpage), www.studentcentre.utas.edu.au/setl
Usher, A (2009), 'University rankings: New frontiers in institutional comparisons', *Australian University Review*, 51(2)
Vaidhyanathan, S (2011), *The Googlisation of Everything (And Why We*

Should Worry), Berkley: University of California Press

Viset, B (2011), 'Unsustainable workloads are an OH&S issue', NTEU, www.nteu.org.au/article/Unsustainable-workloads-are-an-OH-S-issue-11571

Whelan, A, Moore, C, and Walker, R (eds) (2012), *Zombies in the Academy: Living Death in Higher Education*, Bristol: Intellect

Whyte, S (2011), 'Unis hit by foreign student brain drain', *Sydney Morning Herald*, 9 Jan

Willis, P (1977), *Learning to Labour: How Working-Class Kids Get Working-Class Jobs*, New York: Colombia University Press

Wilson, P (2004), 'What is happening to Australian universities?', in Hil and Eddy (eds), *Beyond the Enterprise University*

Winefield, AH, Gillespie, N, Stough, C, Dua, J, and Hapuararchchi, J (2002), *Occupational Stress in Australian Universities: A National Survey*, NTEU

Winefield, T, Boyd, C, Saebel, J, and Pignata, S (2008), 'Update on National University Stress Study', *Australian Universities Review*, 50(1)

Woodward, S (2011), 'ARC inundated with ERA feedback', *Campus Review*, 21(5), p 1

—— (2011), 'US students shirk Australia', *Campus Review*, 21(20), p 7

—— (2011), 'Mental illness on the rise for visiting students', *Campus Review*, 21(23), p 4.